Eat Russian

Eat Russian

Sofka Skipwith
(Née Sofka Dolgorouky)

DAVID & CHARLES : NEWTON ABBOT

0 7153 6187 2

Set in 11 on 13pt Baskerville
and printed in Great Britain
by Latimer Trend & Company Ltd Plymouth
for David & Charles (Holdings) Limited
South Devon House Newton Abbot Devon

To Jack, who tasted

Contents

7

Notes

ALL RECIPES ARE FOR FOUR
UNLESS OTHERWISE STATED

ABBREVIATIONS

tablespoon	tb	gram	g
teaspoon	tsp	kilo gram	kg
ounce	oz	decilitre	dl
pound	lb	litre	l
pint	pt	centimetre	cm
inch	in		

MEASURES

Exact	Approximate as used
1oz = 28g	30g
1lb = 454g	500g
1dl = 3½fl oz	4fl oz
1l = 1¾pt	2pt

1¼ US tb = 1 Imperial tb

9

Oven temperature	Mark	°F	°C
very cool	$\frac{1}{4}-\frac{1}{2}$	250–75	121–35
cool	1–2	300	150
warm	3	325	163
moderate	4	350	177
fairly hot	5–6	375–400	190–204
hot	7	425	218
very hot	8–9	450–75	232–46

Since each oven has its own slight vagaries, the temperature and time of cooking should be adjusted accordingly.

REMARKS

Sugar is used in Russian cooking to bring out flavour in certain products in the same way as salt.

Spices and herbs should never be cooked long as they lose their flavour.

For the same reason pepper should only be added in the last ten minutes of cooking.

Wine to be used in sauces should be boiled for a few minutes before being added to the sauce.

Introduction

Russian cooking is different. It is different not only in the constant use of ingredients such as salted cucumber or sour cream, or in the juxtaposition of contrasting flavours not usual in the west, but above all in what might be termed the 'rhythm of eating'.

The main meal of the day, for instance, called Obed (dinner) is not necessarily either at midday or in the evening. It is a flexible and fluctuating repast, on the timing of which the other meals of the day depend.

If you have dinner in the early afternoon, you would then have a more substantial supper in the evening and finish the day at bedtime with tea, sweet cakes, biscuits etc.

If your dinner is at night, the supper would be changed into lunch. But maybe the dinner is served at 3 pm on return from an 11.30 am matinée at the Bolshoi Theatre. In that case you would adjust your meals accordingly by having a larger breakfast, a snack during the long intervals at the theatre, and a later supper combined with the evening tea. I have, in Moscow, been invited to 'dinner' at the various times of 2 pm, 5.30 and 8.30 . . .

The eating habit of the Russian is roughly as follows: Breakfast is a varied meal with tea or coffee—served after the rest of the meal is eaten—while for the main course you might be offered steak, meat balls or fish, eggs of some kind, stewed fruit, kissel (even caviar), with a plate of different kinds of sweet buns and a platter of bread, as well as various dishes of butter, jam, and honey.

If dinner is to be late then a 'second breakfast' is served about midday consisting of meat and vegetable or a meat or fish 'pirog', perhaps one or two zakouski if any vodka is offered, a sweet or a cottage-cheese dish.

Dinner, whenever it comes, usually starts with zakouski followed by soup accompanied by pirozhki, then a main dish and a sweet.

Should the dinner be early, then supper is served during the evening usually with one hot dish among cold ones such as fish in aspic; fruit tarts; salads or some other dishes taken from the selection of zakouski; sweet cakes and tea.

Afternoon tea was, in pre-revolutionary Russia, the prerogative of the non-working rich, among whom meals followed the western pattern, ie breakfast, lunch, tea and dinner, but with late tea before bedtime instead of the whisky and soda (with soft drinks for the ladies) brought in last thing, as for example in English country houses.

The term 'Russian cooking' is all-embracing. By rights it should refer only to the dishes evolved in the north-western part of a country composed of fifteen republics of which 'Russia' is only one—albeit the most important.

In actual fact 'Russian cooking' incorporates a number of

dishes that have been absorbed from all parts of a country which covers over 8 million square miles and stretches from the east of Europe to the Pacific Ocean at the furthermost end of Asia, from the permafrost of the Siberian tundra to the parched heat of the Caspian deserts.

In 'Russian' cooking Siberian pelmeni, Ukranian borsch, the shashlyks of the Cossacks, caviar produced by sturgeon from the Caspian and spicy soups and pilaffs from Georgia and Armenia are automatically included. A people's way of eating is adapted to suit climatic conditions. Northern peoples living through dark winters of intense cold crave warmth and revitalisation—hence the need for the gulp of spirit with accompanying food typified in Russia by vodka and zakouski, the equivalent of Scandinavian acquavit and smörgasbrod. In the south, spicy foods with herbs and garlic, hot pepper and much fruit are required to titillate the appetite in days of sultry heat, and the food of Transcaucasia is closer to that of the Middle East than of northern Europe. So in Russia, in an area covering over one sixth of the world, each region offers its own style of eating, while certain dishes from all parts have blended into a generally accepted whole.

Foreign influences have barely affected Russian cooking. Some new dishes have been introduced and adopted, such as Beef Stroganov produced in the early nineteenth century by Count Stroganov's French chef, but apart from a few such exceptions the basic cooking has remained unchanged through the centuries. A modern way of life naturally requires modern adaptations, so the working Russian housewife uses meat cubes instead of preparing stock, the flat-dwelling Muscovite takes full advantage of the tinned and frozen foods on sale, as well as of the numerous 'take-away' dishes prepared by restaurants and 'kitchens' in the vast complexes of apartment houses which now ring the old cities. Also, like the British, Russians tend to prefer their own cuisine to any produced abroad.

We know, for instance, that in the eighteenth century the Empress Elizabeth horrified her French chef by insisting on

Russian dishes such as schi (cabbage soup), kouliabiaka (fish in pastry) or Gretchnevaya kasha (buckwheat) being included in the palace menus. In *Daughter of Peter the Great* (1897) by R. N. Bain, one finds the description of an everyday meal in a rich household, at a time when the vast majority of the population had to be satisfied with bread and onion, salt fish and meatless cabbage soup. The meal described could, with very little variation, be offered to a twentieth-century traveller:

> Eat first, if you please, some egg patties with your soup, and then drink hydromel (a form of mead) to wash them down, or else kvass. Pray take a little caviar, the roe of sturgeon. Fish soup you may prefer; cutlets, fowls, game, vegetables are next at your service; and forget not to eat salt cucumber with your roast meat. What do you think of pig and curdled cream? And then apple bread or raw apples from the Crimea or the Siberian or transparent apples, or the Kiev sweetmeat, or honeycomb or preserved rose leaves, or pickled plums . . .

Ever since the sixteenth century when Ivan the Terrible offered gargantuan feasts to his chosen bodyguard, Russians have had the reputation of being hearty eaters. In 1698 Peter the Great came to Britain and is recorded, with his suite of fifteen, to have consumed for supper a side of beef, an entire sheep, three-quarters of a lamb and a leg and shoulder of veal, as well as eight chickens and eight rabbits. They also drank a couple of dozen bottles of sack and a dozen of burgundy, to say nothing of an unmeasured quantity of beer. Modern times have brought even banquets to reasonable proportions, although in June 1972 the papers reported that six men in Azerbaidjan had feasted off two whole sheep and six chickens, consuming between them twenty bottles of vodka and brandy.

In order to provide a rough guide to when various dishes are served, I have split them up according to the different meals at which they are usually found. This is not an inflexible ruling since all the dishes are interchangeable and can be offered at any meal according to circumstances—and appetites.

The following ingredients are those mentioned most frequently in Russian cooking, appearing in every section of the menu from soup to sweet.

Smetana or sour cream

Smetana enriches salad dressing, is the basic ingredient of sauces for fish or meat, and is mixed with fresh fruit in tarts and flans. It is a deliberately and rapidly thickened cream (not a forgotten left-over tasting sour and bitter) and should have a slightly tart flavour but without any acidity. It is easily obtainable commercially.

To prepare at home smetana needs a really hot climte when a bowl of cream set in the sun will thicken by the following day. The cream, of course, should not be pasteurised or contain any preservative. However, cream can be rapidly thickened by the addition of a tablespoon of lemon juice to 5fl oz of cream, or else by using some of the liquid drained from cottage cheese which is mixed with the cream and left overnight in a warm place.

Yoghourt

Yoghourt is to Caucasian cookery what sour cream is to the Russian. It is readily obtainable commercially but easy to make at home. For 2 cups of good milk one needs a dessertspoonful of live yoghourt—or plain dairy yoghourt if the former is unobtainable.

Bring the milk to boiling point and then allow to cool to blood temperature. Beat up the dessertspoonful of culture with a teaspoon and add to the warm milk. Stir several times, transfer to an earthenware bowl, if possible, and cover with a lid. Wrap the bowl in several layers of blanket and leave overnight at room temperature. Before being used it must be chilled in the refrigerator for an hour or two otherwise it is tepid and tasteless if used straightaway after being uncovered. Keep back a dessertspoonful to use as culture for the next batch.

Tvorog

Cottage cheese and curd cheese are the nearest equivalent to the Russian Tvorog which is dry but not 'cheesy'. Curd cheese is best but if unobtainable cottage cheese can be used on condition that all liquid is extracted by draining it for several hours through a cheese-cloth under a heavy weight, and then rubbing it through a sieve to eradicate any lumps. Russians have a variety of uses for tvorog; it is found as a filling in pastry (vatrushki), made into sweet pancakes (syrniki), as the supreme Easter dish (paskha) or in small dumplings in soup. It is delicious as a sweet, sprinkled with cinnamon and eaten with sour cream, or as a savoury mixed with a spoonful of caraway seeds and paprika.

Prostokvasha (sour milk)

Prostokvasha is a favourite and refreshing summer sweet, eaten with sugar and rye bread. It is less bland than yoghourt, being made of fresh cold milk—which should be full cream and unpasteurised. It should not take more than 24hr in a warm place to assume the consistency of junket. A little liquid from the cottage cheese can be used as a 'starter' at the bottom of a bowl of milk. It must be used up as soon as the surface is broken otherwise it separates into buttermilk and curds.

I

Zakouski and Salads

Before the start of the meal a Russian menu invariably includes a variety of zakouski, that distinctive and delicious speciality of the Russian table, which are served with vodka, as appetisers (see p 226).

After each tiny glass of vodka, swallowed at a gulp, some zakouski is eaten to blanket the effect of the spirit. It should be stressed that vodka drunk the Russian way is far less intoxicating than when sipped as a cocktail.

In Russia vodka is usually drunk in unison by the diners to a series of toasts interspersed with zakouski and conversation. The host will raise his glass for the first toast to whatever the occasion, or merely 'good health'. This can be followed by saying 'one leg is lame', then that 'God loves a trinity', followed by 'a house has four corners' and then you can drink to 'the fifth wheel of the cart'.

Zakouski are frequently served on a separate table before going in to the dining-room, when the guests can help themselves. In the famous cookery book, *Podarok Molodoi Khozaike* by Elizaveta Molokhovetz, published at the end of the last century, one finds an illustration of how to arrange a table for zakouski.

On a small square table a revolving tray is set with compartments or small dishes filled with an assortment of zakouski and small slices of white and rye bread. At the sides of the tables are piles of small plates in front of carafes of different vodkas and glasses. Knives and forks are laid in herring-bone pattern from two of the corners leading towards the centre, while from the other two corners—daintily folded napkins. An informal 'Russian party' can consist of a cold buffet of a number of zakouski, with some hot zakouski and bowls of borsch offered some time during the evening. I find that half a dozen or so

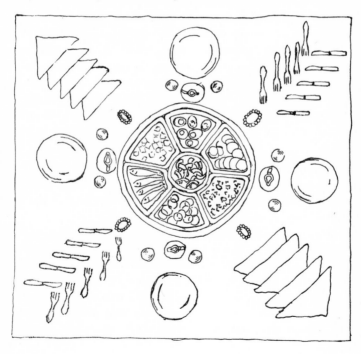

shallow bowls and small oblong dishes are the best way to serve zakouski, since one does not really need more of each than a good tablespoon per person when used as appetisers.

During the last century, in the days of leisurely horse-drawn travel, a hospitable rich country house would have a zakouski table permanently set to revive the unexpected and weary traveller who might decide to break his journey and rest his horses by a stay with friends. At the same time an ever-ready samovar would provide refreshments for the ladies.

Since the essence of zakouski lies in their variety, a full range of recipes follows in order to enable the hostess to ring many changes.

Caviar

Caviar stands alone as the supreme delicacy. There are several kinds of true caviar produced from the roe of the sturgeon. The best—and most expensive—on the market is green-black in colour with every grain rounded. There is a slightly less expensive kind, namely 'pressed caviar', which is darker in colour and its grains are flattened together. Both these, however, are generally far beyond the pocket of the ordinary housewife.

Black caviar can be replaced by an excellent red caviar from the roe of salmon, which is produced in Canada as well as in the Soviet Union. This is about quarter the price of the black variety and the larger grains are often preferred to the more delicate black.

Caviar when served separately, should be very cold. One heaped dessertspoon per portion with the thinnest of hot toast, butter and quarters of lemon.

More economically it is used on small open sandwiches or to decorate canapés or small bouchées of puff pastry with crayfish or prawn filling.

Smoked Salmon

Smoked Salmon too, stands by itself. It is served in wafer-thin slices, sometimes rolled, with brown bread and butter and lemon.

SALADS

Salads are an essential feature of the zakouski table and are more often served as appetisers than, French fashion, as an accompaniment to meat. The following salads however can be used as part of the main course when required. All salads such as cucumber, tomato etc are very popular in Russia but are not included in the following recipes which are of more unusual combinations.

Russian salad

	USA	Imperial	Metric
potatoes, boiled	4	4	4
beetroot (beet), boiled	1 medium	1 medium	1 medium
carrots, boiled	2	2	2
cucumbers, dill pickled	2	2	2
eating apple (or			
soused apple (see p 222))	1	1	1
sauerkraut	1 cup	4oz	120g
spring onion	½ bunch	½ bunch	½ bunch
tomatoes	2 large	2 large	2 large
oil	4 tb	3 tb	3 tb
vinegar — for dressing	2½ tb	2 tb	2 tb
mustard	1 tsp	1 tsp	1 tsp
salt, sugar, to taste			

Peel and dice the cooked vegetables, also the cucumbers and apple, mix with chopped sauerkraut. Make a dressing of mustard, salt and sugar, gradually adding oil and vinegar. Mix the salad with the dressing (or with mayonnaise), sprinkle with chopped spring onion or chives and decorate with sliced tomatoes.

Vinaigrette of fruit and vegetables

	USA	Imperial	Metric
apple	1	1	1
pear	1	1	1
tangerine	2	2	2
orange	2	2	2
potatoes, boiled	4	4	4
carrot	1	1	1
cucumber, fresh	½	½	½
celery	1 stick	1 stick	1 stick
fresh peas	½ cup	2 oz	60g
lemon	½	½	½
mayonnaise	6 tb	5 tb	5 tb
sugar	1 tsp	1 tsp	1 tsp
salt, to taste			

Put aside one orange and one tangerine for decoration. Peel, core, finely dice and mix the remaining fruit and vegetables. Add salt, sprinkle with sugar and stir in the lemon juice. Mix in the mayonnaise, place in a salad bowl and decorate with slices of orange and tangerine. Serve very cold.

Sauerkraut and dried mushroom salad

	USA	Imperial	Metric
mushrooms, dried	2 heaped tb	2 heaped tb	2 heaped tb
sauerkraut	1 lb	1 lb	500g
sour cream	½ cup	4 fl oz	1 dl
salt, pepper, to taste			

Soak the mushrooms for 2–3hr in cold water to cover, boil in the same liquid for 10min, drain and cool keeping the stock. When cold, chop together with the sauerkraut, add both to the mushroom stock, mix in the sour cream and simmer until tender. Drain. Season. Can be served hot or cold.

Platter of assorted cold meats and salami

	USA	Imperial	Metric
varied cold meats	*2lb*	*2lb*	*1kg*
For manikin:			
potato	*1 large*	*1 large*	*1 large*
sweet green pepper	*1 small*	*1 small*	*1 small*
tomato	*1 small*	*1 small*	*1 small*
cocktail sausages	*4*	*4*	*4*

A variety of cold meats may be included, ie roast veal, small lamb chops with the fat trimmed off, rolled slices of ham, tiny meat balls, various salamis, garlic and liver sausage, with a decoration of tomatoes, gherkins or dill pickled cucumbers, button mushrooms, parsley, vegetable salad or any suitable product that is to hand.

To turn this into a party dish prepare a manikin to place in the centre of a round dish as follows:

Into a large halved and washed raw potato stick a skewer leaving the sharp end pointing upwards, so that it stands upright on the potato base. Onto the skewer thread a small green pepper, leaving part of the skewer still sticking out at the top. That forms the body. Fix a small ripe tomato onto the skewer to form the head. Stick in two cloves for its eyes and a couple of long grains of rice for the mouth. A hat made of a leaf, a small flower or a bit of material can be fixed on with a cocktail stick. For the limbs spear four cocktail sausages with sticks and fix them to the 'body'. An olive halved can provide shoes.

Cover the base with lettuce leaves and then arrange the various kinds of meat in lines radiating from the manikin.

Home-made liver pâté

	USA	Imperial	Metric
calves' liver	*1lb*	*1lb*	*500g*
lard	*½ cup*	*4oz*	*120g*
butter	*½ cup*	*4oz*	*120g*

	USA	Imperial	Metric
carrot	*1*	*1*	*1*
onion	*1*	*1*	*1*
parsley with stalk and root	*1 sprig*	*1 sprig*	*1 sprig*
bayleaf	*1*	*1*	*1*
peppercorns	*6*	*6*	*6*
ground nutmeg, a pinch			
salt, pepper, to taste			

Clean the liver of membrane and veins or gristle, cut into small chunks and fry in lard for approximately 4min each side. At the same time fry the diced carrot and onion, with bayleaf, peppercorns and parsley.

When ready, remove the bayleaf and the peppercorns and pass the remainder through the mincer (grinder) twice over. To the minced liver add salt, pepper and a pinch of ground nutmeg, then beat in the butter until no lumps remain. Allow to cool.

The pâté can be served in a dish surrounded by hard-boiled eggs, or else used as a spread on thinly-sliced squares of brown bread, decorated with a touch of tomato purée and a sliver of dill pickle.

Mushroom caviar

	USA	Imperial	Metric
mushrooms, fresh	*½lb*	*8oz*	*240g*
or dried	*4 tb*	*3 tb*	*3 tb*
onion	*1 medium*	*1 medium*	*1 medium*
garlic	*1 clove*	*1 clove*	*1 clove*
celery salt	*1 pinch*	*1 pinch*	*1 pinch*
lemon	*½*	*½*	*½*
paprika	*½ tsp*	*½ tsp*	*½ tsp*
oil	*2½ tb*	*2 tb*	*2 tb*
dill or parsley, to garnish			
salt, to taste			

NOTE: Dried mushrooms should be soaked for a couple of hours before use.

Poach the mushrooms in a little salted water until soft, drain and mince (grind). Chop the onion finely and cook together with a crushed clove of garlic in oil until soft. (Garlic salt could be used if preferred to the clove of garlic.) When cool, add paprika to taste, celery salt, lemon juice and chopped dill or parsley. Dried dill weed can be used if no fresh dill is available, in which case add 1 tsp when cooking the onions. Mix well with the minced (ground) mushrooms and serve very cold as a pâté or else on small squares of buttered bread.

Aubergine or courgette caviar

	USA	Imperial	Metric
aubergines (eggplants) or courgettes (zucchinis) (very young marrows can be used)	2 or 3	2 or 3	2 or 3
onions	2 medium	2 medium	2 medium
tomatoes	2 medium	2 medium	2 medium
oil	2½ tb	2 tb	2 tb
vinegar	2½ tsp	2 tsp	2 tsp
salt, pepper, to taste			

Bake or lightly steam the aubergines (eggplants), remove the skin and the seeds, cut up the flesh adding finely chopped fried onion and peeled fried tomatoes. Stir in salt, pepper, oil and vinegar. Simmer on low heat to evaporate any superfluous moisture. Serve very cold.

Pâté of fresh herring

	USA	Imperial	Metric
good sized herring	1	1	1
unsalted butter	2½ tb	1oz	30g
apple	1 large	1 large	1 large
nutmeg, a pinch			
salt, to taste			
sprig of parsley, to garnish			

Clean, skin and bone the herring carefully, rub the flesh and the butter together through the mincer (grinder). Beat well in a bowl, adding a little nutmeg and salt. On a dish shape the purée into the form of a fish and surround with thinly sliced apple and parsley.

Alternatively the apple can be minced with the herring and butter, in which case the pâté could be served on small squares of brown bread, sprinkling each with parsley.

Salted herring and apple

	USA	Imperial	Metric
salted herring	1	1	1
onion	1	1	1
apple	1	1	1
cream	½ cup	4 fl oz	1 dl
salt	½ tsp	½ tsp	½ tsp
sugar	½ tsp	½ tsp	½ tsp
lemon	½	½	½

NOTE: This dish is also excellent when prepared with kipper fillets.

If the herring is very salt it should be soaked for several hours in water or weak tea. If filleted, soak in milk to give a delicate flavour. The skin and bones should be carefully removed. Join the prepared halves of the fish and cut through into bite-sized pieces. Finely chop the raw apple and onion, add salt, sugar and lemon juice. Mix apple and onion with the cream and cover the fish.

Marinaded fish

Any large white-fleshed fish can be served in this way. The fish should be filleted, skinned, each piece sprinkled with salt and pepper and dipped in flour. Fry, cool and serve covered with the marinade.

	USA	Imperial	Metric
carrots	2	2	2
onions	2	2	2
parsley	bunch	bunch	bunch
oil	5 tb	4 tb	4 tb
tomato purée	5 tb	4 tb	4 tb
bayleaf	1	1	1
peppercorns	3	3	3
ground cinnamon	pinch	pinch	pinch
cloves	5	5	5
vinegar	5 tb	4 tb	4 tb
water	1 cup	$\frac{1}{2}pt$	$\frac{1}{4}l$
sugar, salt, to taste			

Grate the prepared carrots and onion, put in a pan with chopped parsley and oil. Fry gently for 10–15min. Add tomato purée, herbs and spices, cover the pan and simmer for a further 15min. Pour on the vinegar and water, bring to the boil, add salt and sugar and allow to cool.

The fish is placed in a deep dish, the marinade is poured over and it should stand for an hour before serving, sprinkled with chopped dill, parsley or spring onion.

Egg toadstools

> *1 hard-boiled egg per person*
> *half that number of tomatoes, if large, or*
> *1 per egg if medium*
> *potato salad*
> *salt to taste*

Take the required number of hard-boiled eggs, shell and carefully cut off the blunt end so that the egg stands upright on a plate. Select firm ripe tomatoes and cut in half, removing the pips and a little of the flesh. If one end of the tomato is too flat, then use only the top half. Salt the tomato halves and stand in the refrigerator for half an hour. Then pour off the juice from inside the tomatoes and fit them on to the pointed ends of the eggs, to form the cap of the toadstool. Dot the caps with mayonnaise and serve upright on a dish of potato salad, the dressing flavoured with a pinch of tarragon or marjoram.

HOT ZAKOUSKI

Sometimes, especially at official dinners or banquets, zakouski are served when the diners are already seated at table. Caviar is invariably served first, followed by hot zakouski such as a dish of ham in Madeira maybe followed by crab in sour cream sauce, ending with a mushroom, egg and Russian salad. All these are served one after the other during which time toasts are drunk in vodka. The difference between hot zakouski and a main course lies in the size of the portions and in the fact that they are not accompanied by any vegetables. Indeed, unless one first looks at the menu, one can well mistake the zakouski for the meal itself, as happened to me at an official dinner on my first visit to Moscow. I felt I had already had an excellent meal and was fully expecting a soufflé or some ice cream when the soup arrived . . .

Ham in Madeira

	USA	Imperial	Metric
boiled ham, cut thick	½ *slice per person*	½ *slice per person*	½ *slice per person*
flour	½ *tb*	½ *tb*	½ *tb*
butter	1¼ *tb*	1 *tb*	1 *tb*
sour or double (heavy) cream	½ *cup*	4 *fl oz*	1 *dl*
Madeira	6 *tb*	4 *fl oz*	1 *dl*
pepper, to taste			

Quickly brown the ham on both sides in butter, remove from the pan and add the Madeira to the butter. Cook quickly until reduced to about half. Mix in a little flour dissolved in water; when the Madeira is slightly thickened reduce the heat and stir in the cream not allowing it to boil. Replace the ham to heat through, sprinkle with a little pepper and serve.

Sardine butter grill

	USA	Imperial	Metric
sardines	*1 tin*	*1 tin*	*1 tin*
butter	*1 heaped tb*	*1oz*	*30g*
lemon juice	*2½ tsp*	*2 tsp*	*2 tsp*
salt	*½ tsp*	*½ tsp*	*½ tsp*
paprika	*½ tsp*	*½ tsp*	*½ tsp*
tomato purée	*2½ tsp*	*2 tsp*	*2 tsp*
brandy	*2½ tsp*	*2 tsp*	*2 tsp*

Empty the sardine tin with its oil into a bowl, mash the fish and add all other ingredients. Mix thoroughly. Spread thickly onto squares of bread with crusts removed, place under low grill until heated through and browned on top.

Small meat balls in sour cream

	USA	Imperial	Metric
minced (ground) beef	*½lb*	*½lb*	*240g*
bread, without crusts	*2 slices*	*2 slices*	*2 slices*
milk	*2½ tb*	*2 tb*	*2 tb*
onion	*1 medium*	*1 medium*	*1 medium*
oil	*2½ tb*	*2 tb*	*2 tb*
flour	*2½ tb*	*2 tb*	*2 tb*
sour cream	*½ cup*	*4 fl oz*	*1dl*
salt, pepper, to taste			

Soak the bread in the milk, add salt, pepper, the finely minced (ground) beef. Chop the onion very fine and add to the meat. Blend very thoroughly. Take level dessertspoonfuls of the mixture, roll into very small balls, dip in flour and fry quickly on both sides. Pour on the sour cream (ordinary cream can also be used or yoghourt), cover the pan with a lid and simmer for 5—10min on low heat.

Dried mushrooms toasted with cheese

	USA	Imperial	Metric
dried mushrooms	2½ tb	1oz	30g
oil	2½ tb	2 tb	2 tb
flour	½ tb	½ tb	½ tb
sour cream	½ cup	4 fl oz	1dl
onion	1 small	1 small	1 small
grated cheese	2½ tb	1 oz	30g
paprika	½ tsp	½ tsp	½ tsp
salt or garlic salt, to taste			

Simmer the dried mushrooms in water until soft, drain, keeping a little of the liquid. Finely chop the onion and soften in oil. Rub together the flour and the oil, dilute with the mushroom liquid (1 or 2 tb) and the sour cream. Place the mushrooms and onion in a pan, pour on the sauce and simmer on very low heat for 10min. A pinch of garlic salt can be added and ½ tsp paprika.

Fry some rounds of bread in oil lightly on both sides. Heap some of the mushroom mixture on each round, top with grated cheese and put on the top shelf of a moderate oven for 10min.

Forshmak

Forshmak is from the German Vorschmäk (serves 8 for zakouski or 4 for supper). This is an excellent way of using up left-overs, whether the remains of a joint or the boiled meat used for making stock, or else pieces of cold chicken, turkey or game.

	USA	Imperial	Metric
cold meat (beef, veal, lamb or chicken)	½lb	½lb	240g
flour	2½ tb	2 tb	2 tb
boiled potatoes	2–3	2–3	2–3
sour or double (heavy) cream	2½ tb	2 tb	2 tb
eggs, separated	2	2	2
butter, softened	5 tb	4 tb	4 tb

	USA	Imperial	Metric
grated cheese	1¼ tb	1 tb	1 tb
salt herring, previously soaked	½	½	½
salt, pepper, to taste			

Finely chop the cold meat together with the carefully boned herring. Mash the potatoes and add the onion finely chopped and fried. Mix together in a bowl adding flour and softened butter. Stir well and put through the mincer once again. Then add the yolks of the eggs, salt and pepper to taste. Finally fold in the stiffly beaten egg whites, spread evenly in a buttered fireproof dish and sprinkle with grated cheese. Bake in moderate oven for 30min. The forshmak is ready when it comes away from the sides of the dish. Serve hot with a sauce made of sour cream and tomato purée.

Forshmak is often served also as a supper dish. It can be made with any fish instead of meat.

OPEN SANDWICH ZAKOUSKI

Open sandwiches or small savoury squares and rounds of bread are also served as zakouski. These can be made up with various ingredients such as liver pâté with a slice of asparagus; smoked fish with a sliver of dill-pickle cucumber; cottage cheese well drained and mixed with paprika, garlic salt, celery salt and finely chopped gherkin; sardine mashed with chopped parsley and lemon juice and decorated with a blob of tomato purée, etc. To vary open sandwiches various kinds of 'butter' are used which blend or contrast with the other ingredients. These butters are not used with fried bread as that would be too rich a combination.

The following recipes can be used for ½ cup (4oz; 120g) quantity of softened butter.

Mustard butter

Blend with 1 tsp of prepared mustard.

Anchovy butter

2 hard boiled egg yolks
8 anchovy fillets

Pound together the egg yolks and anchovies and add to butter.

Sardine butter

½ can sardines
1 small onion
1 small apple

Soften the grated onion in a little hot water then mash with the fish and grated apple. Blend with the butter.

Cheese butter

Mix the butter with the same amount of grated cheese, 1 tsp of prepared mustard and the yolk of 1 hard-boiled egg.

Ham and egg butter

	USA	Imperial	Metric
ham	¼lb	4oz	120g
egg, hard-boiled	1	1	1
mustard	½ tsp	½ tsp	½ tsp

Mix well the chopped egg and ham, blend with the butter.

Green butter

2 tb finely chopped parsley
lemon juice to taste

Blend with the butter adding a little salt if required.

FRIED BREAD ZAKOUSKI

More unusual are bouchées made with squares or rounds of fried bread. The bread should not be too fresh and should be cut fairly thick so that after being fried in butter, the centre remains soft. Crusts should be removed before frying.

Fried bread and tomato rounds

A slice of tomato is laid on the round of fried bread and covered with a thin layer of mayonnaise to hold the slice of fresh cucumber, topped by a central decoration of a little mayonnaise with either half a black olive or a piece of red radish.

Fried bread, eggs and caviar

A slice of hard-boiled egg is laid on the slightly larger round of fried bread. An edging of butter is placed carefully round the egg while a small mound of caviar ($\frac{1}{2}$ tsp) is arranged in the centre of the yolk.

Fried bread and cheese

The bread can be cut into fancy shapes, (diamond, star, oblong) and a thin slice of cheddar or firm processed cheese is cut to the same shape and fitted over it. In the centre, heap some butter mashed with tomato purée, sprinkle with grated cheese and paprika.

Fried bread and anchovy

Onto a round of fried bread, place first a slice of tomato, then a round of hard-boiled egg topped by a fillet of anchovy arranged in a circle round a little mayonnaise. The anchovy can be replaced by half a sardine cut into 4 strips and placed crosswise over the egg.

c

Fried bread and salmon

On an oval shaped piece of fried bread lay some salmon (fresh or tinned) and cover with mayonnaise to which half a table-spoonful of spinach purée has been added. Decorate with ½ slice of lemon, having removed the pips.

2

Soup

All agricultural communities have found their basic nourishment in soups made from the produce of the land. To this day the farmer's wife in France calls her family to 'la soupe' when dinner is ready. Soup is all the more important in northern climates when it provides warmth as well as food. Thus a soup thick with vegetables made with some meat or lard, when possible, and plentifully accompanied by home-made rye bread would constitute the Russian peasant's main meal of the day. An accompaniment to the daily soup might be a dish of boiled potatoes, eaten with salt and a little butter. (I feel sure that were the potato as rare as asparagus, its elusive flavour would be classed among culinary delicacies. Unfortunately it is too commonplace an item too carelessly cooked to be appreciated as it deserves!)

Over the ages this peasant soup has been altered and refined to suit the more sophisticated taste of town dwellers. That is how soup made of beetroot (beet being one of the main products of central Russia and the Ukraine) has become the internationally renowned borsch.

Equally widespread throughout Russia is 'schi', the basis of which is cabbage, that most common and hardy of all vegetables which, before the days of easy transport, could be grown in the inclement north. The name now extends to cover any soups made with green leafy vegetables such as spinach or sorrel. The extensive use of sauerkraut is also understandable as this was the way cabbage was preserved for the long dark months of winter.

In contrast, a northern summer is short lived but very hot, while in southern Russia the heat is intense. This inclined Russians to cold, spicy soups which are a great feature in their cooking. As autumn approached and the vast forests abounded in wild berries and mushrooms, so developed the taste for soups made of fruit and berries. Mushrooms dried and threaded on strings are extremely popular in soups and sauces. Dried mushrooms taste quite differently from the ordinary mushroom or 'champignon', since they include a large range of varieties.

The abundance of fish in nearby rivers gave birth to 'Oukha', a fish soup as popular as the bouillabaisse of Mediterranean France.

Cucumbers, most beloved of summer salads, also play their part in soups whether fresh or dill-pickled (see p 224), while most western soups such as potato, tomato, green pea or cauliflower also feature widely but their recipes are too well known to be included in the following pages.

The Russian way of serving soup is with a side dish, which ranges from 'pirozhki', buckwheat kasha or cheese toast (grenki) to stuffed hard-boiled egg. Very popular too are clear soups with a variety of tiny stuffed dumplings. A selection of these side dishes can be found on pp 59–64.

STOCK

The use of different stocks is as important to the flavouring of soups as that of later ingredients. Meat or chicken bouillons are most common and in a modern household are frequently replaced by the use of condensed cubes. Fish stock can be prepared from the bones and trimmings of the fish used in the recipe, while mushroom stock is usually made of dried mushrooms which can be bought in most delicatessen. These may appear expensive but since they are extremely light and strongly flavoured only a few are used at a time, making them more economical than at first appears.

If the housewife wants to avoid the several hours cooking needed for a meat and bone stock, minced (ground) meat can be used. That bouillon is ready after an hour's cooking.

Basic meat stock

	USA	Imperial	Metric
beef or chicken	1lb	1lb	500g
carrot	1 large	1 large	1 large
turnip	1 medium	1 medium	1 medium
onion	1 large	1 large	1 large
celery	1 stick	1 stick	1 stick
parsley root	1	1	1
water	3pt	2½pt	1½l
salt, to taste			

Put the meat, and some bones if available, in a saucepan with cold water and leave standing for 20min. Add the vegetables, half of which have been chopped then browned in a frying pan without fat to give colour to the stock. Cook slowly for two to three hours (40min if minced [ground] meat is used) adding salt halfway through the cooking. Strain and use for soup. If allowed to cool the congealed fat can be more easily removed from the surface.

Fish stock

	USA	Imperial	Metric
fish trimmings or whole small fish, fish heads etc	½lb	½lb	240g
onion	1	1	1
carrot	1	1	1
parsley	2 sprigs	2 sprigs	2 sprigs
bayleaf	½	½	½
water	3pt	2½pt	1½l
salt, pepper, to taste			

NOTE: This stock is also used for sauces in fish recipes.

Place the diced vegetables together with the fish in a pan with cold water. Simmer for 1hr adding salt and pepper half way through the cooking. Put in the bayleaf 10min before straining.

Mushroom stock

	USA	Imperial	Metric
dried mushrooms	½oz	½oz	15g
onion	1	1	1
water	3pt	2½pt	1½l
salt, pepper, to taste			

Place the dried mushrooms in a pan with the halved onion, cover with water and leave standing for 1hr to soak the mushrooms (alternatively simmer for 1½hr). When the mushrooms have swelled, cook gently for 30min until they are soft, adding salt and pepper half way through the cooking. Strain the stock. Rinse the mushrooms in cold water and chop finely for use in the soup or in sauce made from the stock. If the stock is too strong it can be diluted with milk or water.

Quantities for soups are calculated for four people reckoning some extra liquid for evaporation or 'second helping'.

BORSCH

Beetroot (beet) that is to be used in soup should always first be cooked very gently in a little water and vinegar, so that the colour is retained, otherwise raw beetroot becomes a greyish pink during cooking. Alternatively, the beet can be cooked whole and only subsequently peeled, chopped and added to the soup. I have given a quick and easy recipe (see p 40) which is a labour saving method but frowned on by the borsch specialists of the different regions, where each method of making the soup varies considerably.

Classic borsch

	USA	Imperial	Metric
meat for stock	*1lb*	*1lb*	*500g*
stock	*3pt*	*2½pt*	*1½l*
beetroot (beet)	*¾lb*	*¾lb*	*350g*
cabbage	*½lb*	*½lb*	*240g*
mixed root vegetables (carrot,			
onion, turnip, parsley root)	*½lb*	*½lb*	*240g*
potatoes	*2 medium*	*2 medium*	*2 medium*
tomato purée	*2½ tb*	*2 tb*	*2 tb*
or fresh tomatoes	*3 medium*	*3 medium*	*3 medium*
sugar	*1¼ tb*	*1 tb*	*1 tb*
vinegar	*1¼ tb*	*1 tb*	*1 tb*
bouquet garni	*1*	*1*	*1*
salt, pepper, to taste			

Prepare meat stock and strain. Simmer the beetroot (beet) cut into fine strips and covered in stock with vinegar added. Put the carrot, onion, turnip, parsley all finely diced into a pan, fry in a little fat from the stock, add the potatoes quartered, tomato purée and sugar. Add the cooked beetroot with its liquid, then add stock. Cover the pan and place on low heat to simmer, stirring occasionally. After 20min add the shredded cabbage and leave to simmer a further 15min. Put in the bouquet garni, salt, pepper, a little more vinegar if required. Simmer 10min or until all vegetables are cooked.

Before serving add the meat from the stock, cut into small pieces with fat carefully removed. Serve with sour cream.

Quick borsch

	USA	Imperial	Metric
cooked salad beets	3 or 4 small	3 or 4 small	3 or 4 small
cabbage	½ head small	½ head small	½ head small
meat stock cubes	3	3	3
potato	1	1	1
onion	1	1	1
tomato purée	1¼ tb	1 tb	1 tb
dried dill weed	pinch	pinch	pinch
bayleaf	small piece	small piece	small piece
sausage	1	1	1
vinegar	2½ tsp	2 tsp	2 tsp
water	3pt	2½pt	1½l
salt, pepper, to taste			

Peel the beets, leaving one aside. Halve and put in pan with water, meat cubes, diced potato, onion, shredded cabbage, sausage cut in small pieces, bayleaf, dill weed and cook for 30min.

Peel the remaining beet, cut in thin strips, cover with cold water and vinegar, leave to stand. This turns a rich red colour.

When the vegetables are cooked remove the large pieces of discoloured beet from the soup, add the bowl of sliced beet

with its water and vinegar; salt and pepper. Heat through
without allowing it to boil and serve with sour cream.

Borsch made with wine

	USA	Imperial	Metric
meat stock	*2pt*	*2pt*	*1l*
beetroot (beet)	*2 medium*	*2 medium*	*1 medium*
white wine	*½pt*	*½pt*	*¼l*
ham	*¼lb*	*¼lb*	*120g*
lemon	*½*	*½*	*½*
parsley, salt, pepper, to taste			

This is an excellent old recipe. The soup is even more delicious
if allowed to stand an hour or two before heating up and
serving.

Bake the raw beets in a hot oven (NOTE: a beet takes a little
longer to bake than a potato of the same size). When cooked
through peel and cut in strips. Put in a pan with wine, lemon
juice, chopped ham and pepper. Add hot stock, salt to taste,
heat through and serve with sour cream.

Malorussian borsch

	USA	Imperial	Metric
ham bone	*1*	*1*	*1*
beef for stock	*½lb*	*8oz*	*240g*
beetroot (beet)	*3 or 4 med*	*3 or 4 med*	*3 or 4 med*
cabbage	*½ small head*	*½ small head*	*½ small head*
vinegar	*2½ tb*	*2 tb*	*2 tb*
bayleaf	*1*	*1*	*1*
flour	*1¼ tb*	*1 tb*	*1 tb*
stock	*3pt*	*2½pt*	*1½l*
salt, pepper, to taste			

Prepare meat stock (see p 37) with the ham bone, bayleaf and
a few peppercorns. An hour before serving put in the cabbage
cut into 4 or 5 pieces, add vinegar and simmer until the cabbage

is tender. Meanwhile wash the beets but do not peel or make any incision in the skin. Boil until soft in water, then peel and cut finely into strips. Take a heaped tablespoon flour and mix with the beet. Add to the stock and cabbage. Salt and pepper to taste. Meat from the stock cut into small pieces or else some diced ham or frikadelki (see p 60) are served in this soup.

Mushroom borsch with prunes

This is prepared exactly like classic borsch (see p 39) except that mushroom stock (see p 38) is used instead of meat stock and a dozen or so prunes are added and cooked in the soup for 20min before serving.

Cold borsch

	USA	Imperial	Metric
beetroot (beet)	*1 lb*	*1lb*	*500g*
boiled potato	*2*	*2*	*2*
cucumber	*1*	*1*	*1*
spring onions	*3*	*3*	*3*
eggs, hard-boiled	*2*	*2*	*2*
sour cream	*1¼ tb*	*1 tb*	*1 tb*
sugar	*1 tsp*	*1 tsp*	*1 tsp*
vinegar	*1¼ tb*	*1 tb*	*1 tb*
horseradish, grated	*1¼ tb*	*1 tb*	*1 tb*
mustard	*¼ tsp*	*¼ tsp*	*¼ tsp*
stock	*3pt*	*2½pt*	*1½l*
salt, pepper, to taste			

Peel the beetroot (beet), dice, put in a saucepan with water. Add 1 tablespoon vinegar and boil for 30min. Strain off the liquid into a basin and chill.

Into a bowl put the diced beet, peeled and diced potato, peeled diced cucumber with seeds removed, chopped eggs and chopped spring onion. Before serving mix in horseradish, salt, sugar and mustard.

Pour on the chilled stock, add sour cream, stir and serve sprinkled with parsley.

SCHI

The name Schi covers all soups made with cabbage or any green leafy vegetable such as sorrel, spinach or young nettles. When sauerkraut is used it should, like beetroot, be braised for 15 or 20 min before adding to the soup as this greatly improves its flavour.

Fresh cabbage schi

	USA	Imperial	Metric
meat for stock	*1lb*	*1lb*	*500g*
cabbage head	*½ small*	*½ small*	*½ small*
mixed vegetables, diced (onion,			
carrot, celery, turnip)	*½lb*	*8oz*	*240g*
tomatoes	*6*	*6*	*6*
potatoes	*2*	*2*	*2*
oil	*2½ tb*	*2 tb*	*2 tb*
bayleaf	*1*	*1*	*1*
stock	*3pt*	*2½pt*	*1½l*
salt, pepper, to taste			

Prepare meat stock (see p 37). Fry in oil diced onion, carrot, celery and turnip. Return to pan with stock and add the chopped cabbage and piece of meat from the stock. Boil for 30min. After 10min cooking put in the quartered potatoes, and 10min before serving add the sliced tomatoes, salt and pepper. Take the meat out of the soup, cut into small pieces carefully removing any fat or gristle and return to the soup. Serve the schi with meat pirozhki (see p 156).

Sour schi

	USA	Imperial	Metric
meat for stock	1lb	1lb	500g
sauerkraut	1lb	1lb	500g
carrot	1	1	1
celery	1 stick	1 stick	1 stick
turnip	1	1	1
tomato purée	2½ tb	2 tb	2 tb
oil	2½ tb	2 tb	2 tb
flour	1¼ tb	1 tb	1 tb
bayleaf	1	1	1
water	2 cup	¾pt	½l
stock	3pt	2½pt	1½l
salt, pepper, to taste			

Prepare a meat stock (see p 37). Place the sauerkraut in a pan with water, oil, cover with a lid and simmer for an hour.

Add stock. Dice and fry the vegetables together with tomato purée, add to the soup and continue simmering for another hour. Ten minutes before serving add bayleaf, salt and pepper. Brown the flour, dilute with a little cold stock, add to the soup and bring to the boil.

Green schi

	USA	Imperial	Metric
spinach (or young nettles)	1lb	1lb	500g
sorrel, chopped	4 cup	8oz	240g
carrot	1	1	1
onion	1	1	1
celery	1 stick	1 stick	1 stick
flour	1¼ tb	1 tb	1 tb
oil	2½ tb	2 tb	2 tb
eggs, hard-boiled	2	2	2
bayleaf	¼	¼	¼
sour cream	½ cup	4 fl oz	1dl
salt, pepper, to taste			

Carefully wash the spinach and cook in boiling water until tender. Drain and rub through a sieve. Keep the water in which the spinach has cooked. Wash the sorrel and chop the large leaves. Fry the chopped onion, carrot and celery in oil in a saucepan, add the flour and brown, stirring for a couple of minutes. Add the spinach also the water in which the spinach cooked, bayleaf and pepper. Cook for 20min. Ten minutes before serving add salt and sorrel leaves. Bring to boil and simmer.

Green schi is served with half a hard-boiled egg on each plate and 1 tb of sour cream.

Young nettles are an excellent substitute for spinach.

Rassolnik

	USA	Imperial	Metric
ox kidney	1lb	1lb	500g
dill-pickled cucumbers	2	2	2
dill-pickle liquid	2½ tb	2 tb	2 tb
parsley roots	2	2	2
celery	1 stick	1 stick	1 stick
onion	1	1	1
potatoes	4 medium	4 medium	4 medium
oil	2½ tb	2 tb	2 tb
chopped sorrel or lettuce	2 cup	4oz	120g
spring onions	3	3	3
sour cream or double (heavy) cream	5 tb	4 tb	4 tb
water	3pt	2½pt	1½l
salt, to taste			

Clean the kidney of any fat, membrane or gristle and cut into fairly large pieces, wash well, place in a pan, cover with cold water and bring to the boil. After a few minutes drain the kidneys, rinse and place in another pan, cover with cold water and simmer for 1½hr.

Dice the onion, carrot, parsley roots and celery; fry gently in oil in the pan in which the soup is to be cooked. When ready take the pan off heat and into it chop the dill-pickled cucumbers and peeled quartered tomatoes. Cover with the strained stock in which the kidneys have been cooking and simmer for another 30min. Ten minutes before serving add 2 tb dill-pickle liquid, the finely chopped sorrel or lettuce, and salt.

On serving, cut the kidney into small pieces and add to the soup which should be accompanied by the cream and finely chopped spring onion.

SOLYANKA

(From the Russian word sol—salt), this is a soup made of either meat, fish or mushroom, but invariably with the addition of dill-pickled cucumbers—called 'slightly salted' in Russian.

Meat solyanka

	USA	Imperial	Metric
meat stock (see p 37)	3pt	2½pt	1½l
assorted cold meat (beef, veal, kidney, tongue, ham, sausages, frankfurters)	½lb	8 oz	240g
dill-pickled cucumbers	4	4	4
onions	2	2	2
tomato purée	1¼ tb	1 tb	1 tb
oil	4 tb	3 tb	3 tb
capers	1½ tb	1 tb	1 tb
stoned olives	12	12	12
sour cream	½ cup	4 fl oz	1dl
lemon	¼	¼	¼
dill or parsley	1 sprig	1 sprig	1 sprig
bayleaf	1	1	1
salt, pepper, to taste			

Chop the onion, fry lightly with the tomato purée and oil and simmer in a little stock. Peel and halve the cucumbers and dice.

Cut the assorted meats in pieces, place in the pan with the onion, and chopped cucumbers, capers, salt, pepper and bayleaf. Pour on the stock and boil for 5–10min. On serving add sour cream, olives, peeled lemon finely chopped, chopped parsley and dill.

Solyanka made with fish

This is prepared exactly as meat solyanka except that the cold meat should be replaced by any white fish carefully cleaned of skin and bone. Salmon makes a very delicate fish solyanka and tinned salmon can well be used. The stock should, if possible, be made with fish (p 38).

Mushroom solyanka

	USA	Imperial	Metric
mushrooms	$\frac{1}{2}lb$	*8oz*	*240g*
dill-pickled cucumbers	*2*	*2*	*2*
onion	*1*	*1*	*1*
capers	*1½ tb*	*1 tb*	*1 tb*
stoned olives	*12*	*12*	*12*
tomato purée	*1¼ tb*	*1 tb*	*1tb*
butter	*1¼ tb*	*1 tb*	*1 tb*
sour cream	*½ cup*	*4oz*	*120g*
lemon	*1*	*1*	*1*
bayleaf	*½*	*½*	*½*
peppercorns	*5*	*5*	*5*
water	*3pt*	*2½pt*	*1½l*
salt, to taste			

Clean and peel the mushrooms, put into a pan with boiling water and simmer for 45min. Remove the mushrooms, set aside and strain the liquid to use as stock.

Soften the chopped onion in butter. When ready add tomato purée and cook a minute or two longer. Peel the cucumbers and dice. Rinse the cooked mushrooms and chop very finely.

47

Place all these ingredients together into the hot mushroom stock, adding capers, peppercorns and bayleaf. Simmer for 10min. Just before serving add the sourcream and heat through, not allowing it to boil.

Into each plate put 3 stoned olives and a small sliver of peeled lemon.

CLEAR SOUPS

The basis of all clear soups is a strong stock made of meat or chicken (see p 37). If cubes are used instead of home-made stock, 1 cube should be reckoned per two portions of soup.

Borschok

	USA	Imperial	Metric
meat stock (see p 37)	3pt	2½pt	1½l
beetroot (beet)	½lb	8oz	240g
white wine	4 tb	3 tb	3 tb
sugar	2½ tsp	2 tsp	2 tsp
salt, pepper, to taste			

The beetroot (beet) should be previously boiled, allowed to cool and then peeled and thinly sliced. Stand it for at least 2hr in the wine (wine vinegar can be used if necessary) sufficiently diluted with water to cover the sliced beetroot. Ten minutes before serving add the beetroot and liquid to the boiling stock together with a spoonful of sugar. Strain.

Serve the soup in cups, accompanied by grenki (see p 63).

Bouillon with baked rice

	USA	Imperial	Metric
clear bouillon (see p 37)	3pt	2½pt	1½l
uncooked rice	½ cup	4oz	120g
eggs	2	2	2

	USA	Imperial	Metric
clarified butter	$1\frac{1}{4}$ tb	1 tb	1 tb
breadcrumbs	$1\frac{1}{4}$ tb	1 tb	1 tb
grated cheese	5 tb	4 tb	4 tb
salt, pepper, to taste			

Boil and drain the rice. Mix in a bowl with the raw eggs, half the butter and half the cheese. Stir well together. Butter a shallow baking tin and sprinkle with half the breadcrumbs. Spread the rice mixture evenly, levelling the surface on to which the remaining breadcrumbs, cheese and butter are sprinkled. Stand on the top shelf of a medium oven to bake.

When well browned allow to cool, then turn out onto a board and cut into squares. Put one square into each soup plate and pour on the hot meat or chicken stock, well strained.

Bouillon and egg

Into each plate of clear bouillon put a shelled egg boiled 'to a bag' ie so that the whites are hard enough to shell but the yolks are soft when broken—6min.

Bouillon and poached omelette

	USA	Imperial	Metric
eggs	2	2	2
milk	$2\frac{1}{2}$ tb	2 tb	2 tb
salt, a pinch			

Beat the eggs in a bowl, add salt and milk. Pour into a small buttered pan, set in a larger one with boiling water, which should then be kept at boiling point without actually boiling. Cover the pan and cook for 15 or 20min until the omelette sets. Allow to cool, cut into squares and place one in each plate of clear bouillon.

A tablespoonful of tomato or spinach purée may be added to the eggs before poaching, if desired.

Bouillon with frikadelki

Prepare the frikadelki as indicated (see p 60). Put 8 or 10 in each plate and cover with clear bouillon.

Bouillon with oushki (see p 62)

Bouillon with klyotski (see p 59)

THICK SOUPS

Cream of lettuce

	USA	Imperial	Metric
lettuce	2–3 large	2–3 large	2–3 large
butter	5 tb	2oz	60g
flour	3½ tb	1oz	30g
milk	2pt	2pt	1l
cream	1pt	1pt	½l
salt, pepper, to taste			

Scald the washed and sorted lettuce leaves for 2min in boiling water. Drain. Mince (grind) the lettuce finely.

Brown the flour in a pan with butter, dilute with hot milk, bring to the boil and add the minced lettuce. Simmer for 15min. Add salt and pepper to taste. Mix in the cream and heat without allowing the soup to boil. Serve with croutons or pirozhki (see pp 154–9).

Cream of liver soup

	USA	Imperial	Metric
liver	1lb	1lb	500g
meat stock (see p 37)	3pt	2½pt	1½l
carrot	1	1	1
leek	1	1	1
onion	1	1	1

	USA	Imperial	Metric
butter	5 tb	2oz	60g
flour	3½ tb	1oz	30g
eggs	2	2	2
milk or cream	½pt	½pt	¼l
salt, pepper, to taste			

Clean the liver of membrane and any hard portions, wash and dice; fry lightly in a pan with the peeled diced vegetables in 1 tb butter. Add a quarter of the stock, salt, cover with a lid and simmer for 40min. Put the liver and vegetables through a fine mincer and then rub through a sieve or liquidise.

Separately heat flour with half the butter, not allowing it to brown, dilute with half the remaining stock, cook for 30min. Strain, stir in the liver purée and the rest of the stock. Bring to the boil adding salt and pepper to taste. Just before serving mix in 2 egg yolks beaten into milk or cream and remaining butter.

Cream of fish with frikadelki

	USA	Imperial	Metric
cod or haddock fillets	1lb	1lb	500g
flour	1¼ tb	1 tb	1 tb
butter	5 tb	2oz	60g
milk	1pt	1pt	¼l
onions	2	2	2
carrot	1	1	1
bayleaf	½	½	½
egg (optional)	1 yolk	1 yolk	1 yolk
water	3pt	2½pt	1½l
salt, pepper, to taste			

Remove the skin and trim the fillets, leaving about a quarter of the fish aside for the frikadelki. Put the skin and trimmings in a pan with sliced onion, carrot, salt and bayleaf and simmer in the water to make fish stock.

Cut the fish into small pieces, simmer with finely chopped onion and 2 tb butter until soft. Add the strained fish stock, cook for a further 20min. When ready rub through a fine sieve or liquidise, add hot milk, salt, pepper, butter. An egg yolk can be mixed with the milk before it is added to the soup.

This soup is served with tiny fish frikadelki made with the unused fish.

Frikadelki: mince (grind) the raw fish, moisten with water, add flour, salt and pepper and form into tiny balls. Drop these into boiling water, when they float up to the surface put 8 or 10 in each plate and cover with the soup.

Cream of crab soup

	USA	Imperial	Metric
crab weighing	*2lb*	*2lb*	*1kg*
or crabmeat	*1 tin*	*1 tin*	*1 tin*
butter	*5 tb*	*2oz*	*60g*
flour	*3½ tb*	*1oz*	*30g*
milk	*1pt*	*1pt*	*½l*
egg yolks	*2*	*2*	*2*
cream	*½ cup*	*4 fl oz*	*1dl*
paprika	*½ tsp*	*½ tsp*	*½ tsp*
salt, to taste			
parsley, to garnish			

Keep aside four large pieces of crab meat and finely mince (grind) the rest. Put in a saucepan, cover with water and simmer for 10min. Separately brown the flour with half the butter, dilute with hot milk, bring to the boil. Into it put the minced crab and stock and simmer for a further 15min. Strain, liquidise or sieve the cooked crab meat, add salt, paprika, butter and beat in the yolks of eggs. Take the pieces of crab cut into squares and add to the soup together with the cream. Sprinkle with chopped parsley. Serve with grenki (see p 63).

Oukha (fish soup)

	USA	Imperial	Metric
fish, mixed (cod, hake, haddock, plaice, sole)	*1lb*	*1lb*	*500g*
water	*3pt*	*2½pt*	*1½l*
onion	*1 medium*	*1 medium*	*1 medium*
leek	*1 large*	*1 large*	*1 large*
parsley (with root)	*1 branch*	*1 branch*	*1 branch*
celery	*1 stick*	*1 stick*	*1 stick*
peppercorns	*10*	*10*	*10*
juniper berries	*10*	*10*	*10*
bayleaf	*½*	*½*	*½*
dry white wine } *optional*	*5 tb*	*4 tb*	*4 tb*
scampi	*½ cup*	*½ cup*	*½ cup*
salt, to taste			

Trim off about a quarter of the fish and prepare a fish stock with the water trimmings and vegetables (see p 38). Strain. Cut the uncooked fish into pieces, put into the strained stock, simmer for 15 or 20min. I find that a few scampi and some dry white wine are an excellent addition. Serve with some pieces of fish in each plate. Oukha is accompanied by rastegai or koulebiaka (see pp 159–61).

Cherry soup with vareniki

	USA	Imperial	Metric
cherries	*1½lb*	*1½lb*	*750g*
flour	*7½ tb*	*2oz*	*60g*
sugar	*2½ tb*	*1oz*	*30g*
eggs	*2*	*2*	*2*
water	*3pt*	*2½pt*	*1½l*

Stone half the cherries. Crush the other half of the cherries in a pan, add the stones from the first half, hot water, sugar, bring to the boil and simmer for 5min. Strain.
Prepare the vareniki: make a stiff dough of flour and beaten eggs, adding a little water if necessary. Roll out thinly on a floured

board and cut into very small rounds. Place a stoned cherry in the centre of each and pinch the edges together. Drop into the hot cherry soup and boil for 10min.

Cold cherry and rice soup

	USA	Imperial	Metric
cherries	½*lb*	½*lb*	*240g*
rice	*4 tb*	*2oz*	*60g*
sugar	*2½ tb*	*1oz*	*30g*
cream	*5 tb*	*4 tb*	*4 tb*
water	*3pt*	*2½pt*	*1½l*

Wash and stone the cherries. Boil the stones for a few minutes in water. Strain. Put the rice and sugar into the cherry-stone stock and simmer for 30min until rice is soft. Five minutes before the end of cooking add the cherries. Cool. Serve very cold with a spoonful of cream on each plate.

Cranberry and apple soup

	USA	Imperial	Metric
cranberries	½*lb*	*8oz*	*240g*
apples	*1lb*	*1lb*	*500g*
sugar	*5 tb*	*2oz*	*60g*
cornflour (cornstarch)	*1½ tb*	*1 tb*	*1 tb*
sour cream	*5 tb*	*4 tb*	*4 tb*
water	*3pt*	*2½pt*	*1½l*

NOTE: When fresh cranberries are unobtainable tinned cranberries can be used instead. In that case only half the sugar is needed.

Crush the cranberries in a pan, add boiling water, cover firmly and simmer for 15min; strain.

Replace on low heat adding sugar and apples, peeled, cored and thinly sliced. When the apples are soft, stir in the cornflour (cornstarch) dissolved in a little cold water. This soup is served cold with a dollop of sour cream in each plate.

Peach and blackcurrant soup

	USA	Imperial	Metric
blackcurrants	½*lb*	½*lb*	*240g*
peaches	*1lb*	*1lb*	*500g*
sugar	*5 tb*	*2oz*	*60g*
cornflour (*cornstarch*)	*1¼ tb*	*1 tb*	*1 tb*
cream	*5 tb*	*4 tb*	*4 tb*
water	*3pt*	*2½pt*	*1½l*

Proceed exactly as for cranberry and apple soup.

COLD SOUPS MADE WITH KVASS

Kvass is a liquid made from fermented rye bread, which resembles a weak beer. It is very popular in Russia, although not to the taste of the western palate, and in summer it is sold in streets and parks by the glass, drawn from the tap of a large barrel-like container with the letters KBAC written large on either side. It is used in the preparation of cold soups where it can be replaced by dry cider. Kvass for drinking at home is made with different flavours (see under Beverages p 227).

Recipe for bread kvass

	USA	Imperial	Metric
rye bread	1lb	1lb	500g
yeast	½pkt	½oz	15g
sugar	½ cup	4oz	120g
raisins	18	18	18
sprig of mint	1	1	1
water	10pt	1gal	5l

Cut the bread into pieces and dry in a very low oven for 1hr. Place the rusks in a large basin and over them pour boiling water. Cover with a cloth and allow to stand for 4hr. Strain the liquid and then add the yeast, sugar and mint. Cover the basin once again and allow 12hr for it to ferment. When the kvass begins to froth strain once again and pour into bottles into each of which 3 raisins have been placed. Cork tightly, with corks soaked in boiling water, tie them down to prevent popping. Leave the bottles racked in a cold place for three weeks, after which the kvass is ready for use.

Okroshka (with meat)

	USA	Imperial	Metric
kvass (see above) or cider	3pt	2½pt	1½l
stock	½pt	½pt	¼l
mixed cooked meats (beef, lamb, veal, ham, tongue)	½lb	8oz	240g
cucumber (fresh or dill-pickle)	1	1	1
spring onions	2	2	2
eggs, hard-boiled	2	2	2
sour cream	5 tb	4 tb	4 tb
sugar	1 tsp	1 tsp	1 tsp
salt, to taste			
mustard, to taste			
parsley, dill, tarragon, to garnish			

Peel the cucumber and dice together with the meat; chop the spring onion and crush in a plate adding a little salt (this will soften the onion). Chop the whites of the shelled eggs. Rub the yolks in the soup tureen with mustard, sugar and salt. Put the meat, cucumber and onion into the tureen and pour on kvass and stock. Sprinkle with finely chopped dill and tarragon (or parsley) and stand in the refrigerator for ½hr before serving. Into each plate place a cube of ice and a portion of sour cream.

Mixed vegetable okroshka

	USA	Imperial	Metric
kvass (see p 56) or cider	3 pt	2½pt	1½l
meat or mushroom stock	1pt	1pt	½l
boiled potatoes	2	2	2
cooked beetroot (beet)	1 small	1 small	1 small
dill-pickled cucumbers	2	2	2
fresh or soused apple	1	1	1
spring onions	3	3	3
eggs, hard-boiled	2	2	2
sugar	1 tsp	1 tsp	1 tsp
mustard	½ tsp	½ tsp	½ tsp
sour cream	2½ tb	2 tb	2 tb
salt, to taste			

NOTE: Marinaded plums, cherries, grapes can be added, also any other cooked vegetables such as cauliflower, cabbage, turnip, mushrooms fresh or marinaded.

Cut the cooked potatoes into slices and dice all other cooked chilled vegetables, cucumbers and apple. Finely chop the spring onion and crush with a spoon to soften and bring out the juice, adding a little salt. Shell the eggs, chop the whites and crush the yolks in mustard.

Mix the sliced potato and onion, yolks, sour cream, sugar; salt to taste. Pour on kvass and stock, add diced vegetables, and mushrooms from the stock (if used). Cool in refrigerator. Serve with a cube of ice on each plate.

Botvinya with fish

	USA	Imperial	Metric
kvass (see p 56) or cider	3pt	2½pt	1½l
stock	½pt	½pt	¼l
spinach	½lb	8oz	240g
sorrel	½lb	8oz	240g
cucumber	1	1	1
spring onions	3	3	3
grated horseradish	2½ tb	2 tb	2 tb
cooked white fish or crayfish	½lb	8oz	240g
mustard	¼ tsp	¼ tsp	¼ tsp
dill or parsley			
salt, to taste			
sherry or champagne (optional)			

Wash the spinach and cook in a little boiling water. Wash the sorrel and steam separately in a closed saucepan. Drain both and rub through a sieve. Put this purée into a bowl, add sugar, salt, mustard and mix with kvass and stock.

Chill the soup in the refrigerator also the cooked fish or crayfish carefully cleaned of skin and bones. On serving put some fish in each plate, sprinkle with grated horseradish, cover with soup. At the last minute put some crushed ice in each plate. Sprinkle with chopped parsley.

If desired a small glass of sherry or a little champagne can be added to the soup just before serving.

Kholodetz (also known as khlodnik)

	USA	Imperial	Metric
kvass or cider	1pt	1pt	½l
stock	1½pt	1½pt	1l
young beet with its leaves	1lb	1lb	500g
cucumber	1	1	1
spring onions	3	3	3
eggs, hard boiled	2	2	2

	USA	Imperial	Metric
sour cream	$2\frac{1}{2}$ tb	2 tb	2 tb
sugar	$1\frac{1}{4}$ tb	1 tb	1 tb
salt, to taste			
parsley, to garnish			

Wash and peel the beet, place in a pan with the stock. Cook for 30min. Ten minutes before the time elapses add the sorted and washed beet leaves, and salt. When ready drain off the liquid and chill. Chop the beets finely, mix with chopped eggs, diced cucumber, chopped spring onion. Add sour cream and sugar. Pour on kvass and chilled beet stock. Serve sprinkled with chopped parsley.

ACCOMPANIMENTS TO SOUP

Klyotski made with flour

	USA	Imperial	Metric
flour	1 cup	4oz	100g
butter	$1\frac{1}{4}$ tb	$\frac{1}{2}$oz	12g
stock (water)	$\frac{1}{2}$ cup	4 fl oz	1dl
egg	1	1	1
salt	$\frac{1}{2}$ tsp	$\frac{1}{2}$ tsp	$\frac{1}{2}$ tsp

Put the stock in a bowl with melted butter, beaten egg and salt. Mix well gradually adding the flour, to form a stiff dough. Take 1 tb and with the help of a teaspoon separate off small oval portions. Drop into boiling stock or water until the klyotski float to surface. Serve in the plate of bouillon.

Semolina klyotski

	USA	Imperial	Metric
semolina	1 cup	4oz	120g
butter	$2\frac{1}{2}$ tb	2 oz	30g
eggs	2	2	2
salt	$\frac{1}{2}$ tsp	$\frac{1}{2}$ tsp	$\frac{1}{2}$ tsp
stock	$\frac{1}{2}$ cup	4 fl oz	1dl

Into a pan put stock, butter, salt and bring to the boil. Gradually add semolina, stirring well; cook for 5 or 6min until very thick. Take the pan off heat, add beaten eggs and proceed as for previous recipe.

Potato klyotski

	USA	Imperial	Metric
potatoes	*3 large*	*3 large*	*3 large*
butter	*4 tb*	*2oz*	*60g*
eggs	*2*	*2*	*2*
salt	*½ tsp*	*½ tsp*	*½ tsp*

Peel and boil the potatoes, mash while hot. Add raw egg yolks, salt and butter, mix well. Beat the whites until fluffy and fold carefully into the potato mixture. Proceed as for klyotski made with flour.

Frikadelki

Frikadelki are tiny balls prepared of raw meat or chicken. Whatever the mixture, frikadelki should be no larger than a small walnut. They must be dropped into boiling water in a separate pan some 15min before serving the soup and cooked gently on low heat for 10min, without allowing the water to boil, otherwise they are apt to disintegrate. When they float up to the surface remove with a perforated spoon, put a few into each soup plate and allow to cool slightly before covering with hot bouillon.

Meat frikadelki

	USA	Imperial	Metric
meat, finely minced (ground)	*½lb*	*½lb*	*240g*
salt, pepper, to taste			

Mix the finely minced meat with salt, pepper and a spoonful of

cold water so that it sticks together when formed into tiny balls.
Cook as specified above.

Chicken frikadelki

	USA	Imperial	Metric
chicken, chopped	1 cup	4oz	120g
egg white	1	1	1
white bread	thick slice	thick slice	thick slice
milk	5 tb	4 tb	4 tb
salt, pepper, to taste			

Soak the crustless bread in the milk and squeeze dry. Mince
the raw chicken meat finely and mix well with the bread.
Add white of egg and beat till blended and the mixture assumes
an even consistency. Add salt and pepper. Rub through a fine
sieve, if necessary, to remove any lumps. Form into tiny balls
and cook as specified.

Kidney frikadelki

	USA	Imperial	Metric
lamb's kidneys	2	2	2
onion	1 medium	1 medium	1 medium
eggs	2	2	2
cream or sour cream	2½ tb	2 tb	2 tb
butter	1¼ tb	½oz	15g
breadcrumbs	7½ tb	6 tb	6 tb
salt, pepper, to taste			
nutmeg, a pinch			

Put the kidneys into boiling water and bring twice to the boil.
Drain, rinse, remove membrane, fat and core, cut up finely and
salt. Chop the onion, soften in butter, mix with the kidney
and half the breadcrumbs. Beat together eggs, cream and a
little pepper. Add to kidneys and mix to a stiff paste, adding
salt and nutmeg. Form into small balls, roll in breadcrumbs.
Cook as specified.

Cheese frikadelki

	USA	Imperial	Metric
cheese, grated	1 cup	4oz	120g
butter	2½tb	2tb	2tb
eggs	2	2	2
bread	2 slices	2 slices	2 slices
milk	1¼ tb	1 tb	1 tb
cream	1¼ tb	1 tb	1 tb
breadcrumbs	2½ tb	2 tb	2 tb
salt, pepper, to taste			

Mix together the grated cheese and softened butter till blended. Beat the eggs. Soak the bread in milk and squeeze dry; add cream and mix well with the cheese and butter, adding salt and pepper to taste. The mixture should have the consistency of a stiff dough. Make tiny balls and cook as specified.

Oushki

Oushki are little dumplings with a meat or mushroom filling. Pastry for oushki is rolled out very thinly and cut into little squares. Place some filling in the centre, smear the edges with white of egg and fold over in a triangle. Pinch the edges together very firmly. These can be boiled or fried in oil or butter and then allowed to drain and dry. A few are placed in the soup plates just before serving and covered with hot bouillon. This should be done at the very last moment so that the oushki do not become soggy from the liquid.

Oushki with meat

	USA	Imperial	Metric
minced (ground) beef or pork (or ½ each)	1 cup	6oz	180g
onion	1 small	1 small	1 small
flour	1 cup	4oz	120g
egg	1	1	1

	USA	Imperial	Metric
egg, hard-boiled	*1*	*1*	*1*
(*optional*)			
salt, pepper, to taste			

Mince (grind) the meat and onion together, add a little water, pepper and salt, mix very thoroughly. A chopped hard-boiled egg can be added.

Prepare a stiff dough with flour and egg, adding salt and a little water if required. Roll out thinly on a floured board and cut out small squares. Place a little meat filling on each, fold over and pinch sides together. Drop into boiling water, simmer for 10min till they float to the surface, remove with a perforated spoon and serve in plates with bouillon or fry as specified in 'remarks'.

Oushki with mushroom

Prepare as for oushki with meat (above) but instead of meat use the same amount of chopped mushroom.

Grenki

Grenki are small squares of bread, one side covered with grated cheese and sprinkled with butter. They are laid on a baking sheet and placed in the oven until the cheese is melted and browned, or else are roasted under a grill.

Stuffed eggs in shells

	USA	Imperial	Metric
eggs, hard-boiled	½ *per person*	½ *per person*	½ *per person*
butter	*1 tb*	½*oz*	*15g*
breadcrumbs	*2½ tb*	*2 tb*	*2 tb*
egg, raw	*1*	*1*	*1*
parsley	*1 sprig*	*1 sprig*	*1 sprig*
salt, pepper, to taste			

Cut cold hard-boiled eggs lengthwise with a very sharp knife so as not to damage the shells. Carefully remove egg from shell, chop finely, put in pan with melted butter, breadcrumbs, chopped parsley and a raw egg. Mix very thoroughly and fill each half shell with the mixture. Sprinkle with breadcrumbs, dot with butter, brown under the grill.

3
Fish

'The rivers of Russia have, from remote antiquity, been the true channels of trade and migration and have contributed much more to the elaboration of national unity than any political institution', wrote Kropotkine in 1888.

Villages grew up along the banks of the rivers and their inhabitants found an almost inexhaustable supply of fish in the deep waters. The most important of all Russian rivers is the Volga, which winds from north-west Russia for 2,325 miles until it falls into the Caspian Sea. It is by far the longest river in Europe—the Rhine, for instance, is only 825 miles long and the Danube 1,735 miles.

The Volga basin with its hundred odd tributaries covers over half a million square miles—an area as large as England, France and Germany put together. That is why in old Russian cuisine river fish played a far greater role than sea fish. The Volga abounds in several species of sturgeon, which travel 250 miles up river to spawn. These are followed by numerous shoals of roach and trout and salmon. There are huge pike and bream and vast numbers of herring from the Caspian, to say nothing of lamprey, sterlet, tench and gudgeon. Once again to quote Kropotkine, who gives a picture of the fishing industry that employed some 70,000 people round the Volga estuary at the turn of the century:

> From the end of June onwards immense trawl nets, sometimes a mile long, are continually at work, occasionally taking at one haul as many as 40,000 bream, 150,000 roach and 200,000 herring. It is estimated that 180,000 tons of fish are taken annually from the four fishing districts of the Caspian.

Today, with modern transport and refrigeration, cod from the White Sea, sole, haddock, mackerel and hake all add to the great variety of fish, fresh and tinned, sold throughout the Soviet Union. Before modern methods were in use fish had to be dried and salted for the winter, when rivers were frozen over with thick ice and served as highways for horse-drawn sleighs. Thus an old cookery book says about cod:

> This is an extremely tasty fish but can only be eaten where it is caught. It is very delicate and cannot be transported fresh, that is why cod is always immediately salted . . .

Cod with dill-pickled cucumber

	USA	Imperial	Metric
cod fillets	1½lb	1½lb	750g
dill-pickled cucumbers	2	2	2
dill-pickle liquid	1 tb	1 tb	1 tb
mushrooms, chopped	2 tb	1oz	30g

	USA	Imperial	Metric
white sauce	*1 cup*	*6oz*	*180g*
white wine	*2 tb*	*2 tb*	*2 tb*
butter	*2 tb*	*1oz*	*30g*
salt, pepper, to taste			
parsley, to garnish			

Simmer the fillets in a little water with 1 tb of dill-pickle solution. Peel cucumbers, remove seeds, and simmer the quarters together with the fish. Lightly fry chopped mushrooms. Make a white sauce using the liquid in which the fish was poached and add white wine.

Lay mushrooms and cucumbers onto each fish fillet and cover with sauce. Sprinkle with chopped parsley.

Stuffed fillets of cod with crayfish sauce

	USA	Imperial	Metric
fillet of cod	*1lb*	*1lb*	*500g*
mushrooms, chopped	*1½ cup*	*4oz*	*120g*
crayfish tail or	*1*	*1*	*1*
prawns	*8*	*8*	*8*
white breadcrumbs	*2 cup*	*4oz*	*120g*
milk	*5 tb*	*4 tb*	*4 tb*
egg white	*1*	*1*	*1*
cream	*1¼ tb*	*1 tb*	*1 tb*
stock	*1 cup*	*8 fl oz*	*2dl*
flour	*1¼lb*	*1 tb*	*1 tb*
salt, pepper, to taste			

Remove the skin from the fillets, trim. With the skin and trimmings make stock. Mince (grind) half the fish and cut the remaining fillets into thin strips on which spread the filling prepared as follows: soak the crustless bread in milk, mix with the minced fish. Add egg white and beat thoroughly till the mixture becomes light and fluffy, gradually adding the tablespoonful of cream. Finally add salt and pepper.

Spread thickly on the strips of fish, roll up and put into a casserole, pour on the fish stock and cover tightly with a lid. Braise for 15min in a hot oven.

Crayfish sauce Thicken the fish stock with flour and add chopped mushrooms and pieces of crayfish lightly fried. Serve over the rolled fillets.

Cod steaks with caraway cabbage

	USA	Imperial	Metric
cod steaks	4	4	4
cabbage, chopped	2 cup	8oz	240g
flour	1¼ tb	1 tb	1 tb
oil	2½ tb	2 tb	2 tb
butter	1 tb	½oz	15g
caraway seeds	1 tsp	1 tsp	1 tsp
sugar	1 tsp	1 tsp	1 tsp
red sauce (see p 85)	5 tb	4 tb	4 tb
spring onion, to garnish			
salt, pepper, to taste			

Sprinkle the fish with salt and pepper, dip in flour and brown on both sides in oil. Shred and gently braise the cabbage in oil until soft. Scald the caraway seeds in boiling water to soften and mix with the cabbage together with 1 tsp of sugar.

Place a layer of cabbage into a casserole, on it lay the cod steaks, cover with another layer of cabbage. Pour on the red sauce and simmer for 15min.

To serve, place a cod steak on a plate, cover with cabbage, top with some sauce and sprinkle with chopped spring onion.

Sole with leeks and apples

	USA	Imperial	Metric
fillet of sole	8	8	8
apples	4 large	4 large	4 large
leeks	4 small	4 small	4 small
white wine	5 tb	4 tb	4 tb

	USA	Imperial	Metric
sour cream	5 tb	4 tb	4 tb
butter	2½ tb	2 tb	2 tb
salt, pepper, to taste			

NOTE: Plaice, lemon sole and flounder can be prepared in the same way.

Peel, core and slice the apples; chop the white parts of leeks; mix and place in a buttered casserole and on them lay the fillets of fish. Add salt and pepper. Pour on white wine with same amount of water or fish stock made from the skin and trimmings of the fish. Simmer gently, basting the fish occasionally with the liquid. When the fish is cooked, keep warm while rapidly reducing the liquid to half. Mix in sour cream (fresh double [heavy] cream can be used) and pour over the fish.

Sole in red wine

	USA	Imperial	Metric
fillets of sole	8	8	8
onion	1	1	1
red wine	1 wineglass	1 wineglass	1 wineglass
butter	5 tb	2oz	60g
flour	1¼ tb	1 tb	1 tb
cloves	4	4	4
parsley	1 sprig	1 sprig	1 sprig
stock	1 cup	½pt	¼l
bayleaf	¼	¼	¼
salt, pepper, to taste			

Chop parsley and onion, put into a pan with cloves, bayleaf and pepper. Salt the fish, cut each fillet in half and lay on top of the onion. Pour on red wine and stock, cover the pan and simmer for 20min. Pour the liquid off into another pan and reduce rapidly to half. Rub together flour and butter, add to the reduced liquid and simmer for 3min until thickened. Remove sauce off heat, add a little butter and stir well till blended. Season to taste, strain and pour over the fish.

Sole stuffed with shrimps

	USA	Imperial	Metric
sole	2 or 4 small	2 or 4 small	2 or 4 small
breadcrumbs	7½ tb	6 tb	6 tb
parsley, chopped	1 tb	1 tb	1 tb
butter	6 tb	3 oz	90g
shrimps	small tin	small tin	small tin
egg	2	2	2
nutmeg, a pinch			
salt, pepper, to taste			

NOTE: Plaice, flounder, bream or bass can be used.

Select good sized fish and make an incision along either side of the backbone. Prepare a stuffing of breadcrumbs, butter, chopped parsley, chopped shrimps mixed together with beaten egg, nutmeg, salt and pepper.

Lay the stuffing along the bone, under the fillets, leaving the centre open. Brush the fish with beaten egg, sprinkle with breadcrumbs and bake in a buttered dish in a hot oven for 20min, until well browned.

Fillets of sole with spinach

	USA	Imperial	Metric
fillets of sole	8	8	8
spinach	1lb	1lb	500g
white wine	7½ tb	6 tb	6 tb
white sauce	1 cup	8 fl oz	2dl
grated cheese	½ cup	4oz	120g

NOTE: This dish can be prepared with any filleted fish.

Simmer the fillets in wine and cook the prepared spinach very gently in butter. Place the spinach in a buttered dish with the fillets on top. Cover with thick white sauce which in turn should be topped by a layer of grated cheese and dotted with butter. Place in a hot oven or under a grill until the cheese is well browned.

Salmon in Madeira

	USA	Imperial	Metric
salmon steak	4	4	4
butter	½ cup	4oz	120g
Madeira	5 tb	4 tb	4 tb
bayleaf	½	½	½
salt, to taste			

Melt the butter in a pan, add Madeira and bayleaf, bring to the boil. Salt the salmon steaks and place in the Madeira. Simmer on low heat for 20min. Serve with a crayfish sauce (see p 68).

Salmon with cherry sauce

	USA	Imperial	Metric
salmon	1½lb	1½lb	750g
stock	10 tb	8 tb	8 tb
white wine	5 tb	4 tb	4 tb
bayleaf	½	½	½
salt, to taste			

Put the salmon in a pan with the other ingredients and simmer without hard boiling for 40min, if necessary adding stock. When cooked cover with sauce given in the next recipe and serve.

Cherry sauce

	USA	Imperial	Metric
cherry syrup	5 tb	4 tb	4 tb
port	5 tb	4 tb	4 tb
cloves	4	4	4
cinnamon	½ tsp	½ tsp	½ tsp
olives, stoned	12	12	12
sugar lumps	2	2	2
olive oil	1¼ tb	1 tb	1 tb
fish stock	1 cup	8 fl oz	2dl

	USA	Imperial	Metric
lemon	½	½	½
butter	5 tb	2oz	50g
flour	1¼ tb	1 tb	1 tb

In a small frying pan brown the sugar, add 2 tb of stock, bring to the boil and pour into a saucepan with olive oil and butter. Brown the flour and dilute with the rest of the fish stock. Add to the pan with port, cherry syrup. Stir and put in cloves, cinnamon, juice of ½ lemon. Cook, gently stirring all the time until the sauce thickens. Strain and add the chopped olives. Bring once to the boil and serve.

Tinned salmon in white wine

	USA	Imperial	Metric
salmon	1 tin	1 tin	1 tin
white wine	1 wineglass	1 wineglass	1 wineglass
mushrooms	½lb	8oz	240g
butter	5 tb	2oz	60g
flour	1¼ tb	1 tb	1 tb
egg yolk	1	1	1
salt, to taste			

Chop and lightly fry the mushrooms then put in a pan with the tinned salmon. Mix the liquid from the tin with wine, pour over the mushrooms, cover with a lid and allow to heat through for 5 or 6min. Take out the fish and keep hot. Rub the flour with 1 tb of butter, add to the pan, stir until well blended and allow to boil for a few minutes. Remove the pan from heat, mix in the egg yolk beaten with 2 tb of softened butter; stir, add salt and strain. Before pouring over the fish heat up the sauce. Serve with fingers of fried bread.

Salmon, sturgeon or halibut barbecued

	USA	Imperial	Metric
fish	2lb	2lb	1kg

	USA	Imperial	Metric
tomatoes	12	12	12
onion	1	1	1
butter	5 tb	2oz	60g
salt, pepper, to taste			

Cut the fish into about 8 pieces, rinse in cold water and sprinkle with salt and pepper, thread onto a spit. Cook over glowing charcoal for 10min, constantly turning and brushing the fish with butter. On a separate spit cook whole tomatoes, 3 per person. To serve take the pieces of fish off the spit, put on each plate with the tomatoes and sprinkle with finely chopped raw onion.

Trout in white wine

	USA	Imperial	Metric
trout	4	4	4
white wine	½ bottle	½ bottle	½ bottle
butter	½ cup	4oz	120g
lemon	1	1	1
salt, to taste			

Scale, wash and dry the fish. Salt and place in a fish pan. Pour on sufficient wine to half cover the fish, add the butter and slices of lemon with pips removed. Cover the pan firmly and cook on medium heat for 15min. This excellent dish can be easily prepared on a camping stove or on a heater at table.

Zrazy (fish fillets stuffed with mushroom)

	USA	Imperial	Metric
fish, trout, haddock or cod	8 small or 4 large fillets	8 small or 4 large fillets	8 small or 4 large fillets
mushrooms	½lb	8oz	240g
butter	½ cup	4oz	120g
onion	1	1	1
parsley	2 sprigs	2 sprigs	2 sprigs

	USA	Imperial	Metric
egg yolks	*2*	*2*	*2*
flour	*1¼ tb*	*1 tb*	*1 tb*
lemon	*½*	*½*	*½*
cream	*½ cup*	*4 fl oz*	*1dl*
salt, pepper, to taste			

Lay fish fillets flat, skin down, trim edges, remove any remaining bones, moisten with cold water and beat flat with a cleaver. Sprinkle with salt and pepper and spread with stuffing—see below. Turn in the edges of the fish on all sides, roll into tubes and arrange these, opening downwards in a deep well-buttered pan. Fry gently on low heat for 10min until the surface hardens.

Make stock from the bones and trimmings and strain. Pour half onto the fish so that it comes three-quarters way up the zrazy. Cover the pan and simmer for 10min.

Stuffing Fry the chopped mushrooms, onion and parsley in a little butter, add salt, pepper and 1 tsp of water to bind. Mash together.

Sauce Take the remaining fish stock and bring to boil. Blend flour with the same amount of butter, gradually dissolve in the boiling stock, mix until absolutely smooth. Add half the cream and (optional) a little mushroom essence. Bring to the boil and pour over the zrazy. Allow to simmer for 5min. Just before serving put the beaten egg yolks into the pan with the remaining cream. Boil once, take off heat and add the sauce from the zrazy pan. Mix until absolutely smooth. Heat, stirring, without allowing it to boil, add salt and lemon juice. Strain onto the fish zrazy laid ready to serve on a hot dish.

Eel in red wine

	USA	Imperial	Metric
eel	*2lb*	*2lb*	*1kg*
onion	*2*	*2*	*2*
lemon	*1*	*1*	*1*
red wine	*½ bottle*	*½ bottle*	*½ bottle*
salt, to taste			

Put chopped onion, lemon juice and wine in a saucepan and bring to the boil. Cut the eel into pieces, salt and put into the pan. Boil rapidly until the sauce is reduced by half and the eel is cooked. Serve with the sauce and onion.

Baked minced (ground) eel

	USA	Imperial	Metric
eel	*2lb*	*2lb*	*1kg*
bread, white	*4 cup*	*8oz*	*240g*
onion	*1*	*1*	*1*
eggs	*2 small*	*2 small*	*2 small*
butter	*2 tb*	*1oz*	*30g*
sour cream	*2 tb*	*2 tb*	*2 tb*
mushrooms, chopped	*1 cup*	*4oz*	*120g*
breadcrumbs, as required			
salt, pepper, to taste			

Skin the eel and remove flesh from backbone, being careful not to break it. Mince the flesh and mix with the bread soaked in a little water and squeezed dry; finely chop and lightly fry the onion, add to eel mixture with salt and pepper. Mix in the eggs, not allowing the mixture to become too moist. Finally add the chopped mushrooms and sour cream. Surround the backbone with the firm mixture in the shape of an eel, roll in breadcrumbs and lay carefully in a buttered dish to bake for 15 or 20min in a hot oven, basting frequently with melted butter. Serve with a sharp hollandaise sauce (see p 84).

Pike or hake barbecued

Pike is a favourite fish in Russia, as it is found in most of the rivers. It is prepared in many ways—boiled, baked, minced (ground)—and served with a variety of sauces. Hake is the nearest equivalent in sea fish.

A favourite way is to cook it over charcoal, the whole fish being threaded on a spit and larded with thin strips of pork fat, tied on round the fish. It should be well basted with butter while cooking and served with a salad.

Pike or hake with saffron sauce

	USA	Imperial	Metric
fish	*2lb*	*2lb*	*1kg*
white wine	*1 cup*	*8 fl oz*	*2dl*
vinegar	*2½ tb*	*2 tb*	*2 tb*
carrot	*1*	*1*	*1*
celery	*1 stick*	*1 stick*	*1 stick*
leek	*1*	*1*	*1*
peppercorns	*10*	*10*	*10*
raisins	*1 cup*	*6oz*	*180g*
onions	*2 medium*	*2 medium*	*2 medium*
flour	*1 cup*	*4oz*	*120g*
ground saffron	*½ tsp*	*½ tsp*	*½ tsp*
sugar	*2½ tb*	*1oz*	*30g*
lemon	*½*	*½*	*½*
butter	*2½ tb*	*1oz*	*30g*
salt, to taste			

Cut the fish into pieces, salt and leave for an hour. Place in a saucepan and pour on wine and vinegar, adding enough water to cover the fish. Boil carrot, celery, leek and onion, chop and add to the pan with fish, also raisins, sliced lemon with pips removed. Boil rapidly for 15min until fish is cooked.

Saffron sauce for fish   The sauce is prepared as follows: in a separate pan mix butter, flour, sugar and saffron with 8 tb liquid from the fish pan. Simmer, stirring until the sauce thickens. Strain over the fish laid on a hot dish. Drain the vegetables, lemon and raisins from the cooking and place these round the fish.

Fish with horseradish

	USA	Imperial	Metric
fish	2lb	2lb	1½kg
white bread	2 cup	4oz	120g
breadcrumbs	1 cup	2oz	50g
milk	2½ tb	2 tb	2 tb
grated horseradish	½ cup	4oz	120g
egg, hard-boiled	3	3	3
egg white	1	1	1
egg yolk	2	2	2
butter	5 tb	2oz	50g
sour cream	1 cup	8 fl oz	2dl
nutmeg	1 pinch	1 pinch	1 pinch
salt, pepper, to taste			

NOTE: Suitable for pike, hake, bream, cod or haddock.

Remove skin and any bones from the fish, rub it over with salt and cut into suitable pieces. Make forcemeat with a third of the fish, ie chop it very finely with hard-boiled eggs, salt, pepper and a pinch of nutmeg. Add 1 tb of butter, the raw white of egg and the crustless bread soaked in milk. Stir well together and rub through a fine sieve.

In a small deep casserole melt 1 tb of butter and spread half the fish in a layer. Brush the fish with butter and raw yolk and bake in a hot oven for 15min. Take out of the oven, brush with butter, sprinkle with a layer of breadcrumbs and grated horse-radish and return for a few minutes to the oven for the bread-crumbs to bake. Then spread on a layer of the prepared force-meat and put back in the oven for 10min to harden the surface. Cover the forcemeat with a further layer of fish, brush with butter and egg yolk and cover with a layer of breadcrumbs and horseradish also dotted with butter. Bake in the oven for 10min. Finally pour on the sour cream and leave a few more minutes in the oven to heat through. Serve in the casserole.

Carp in ale

	USA	Imperial	Metric
carp	1 small	1 small	1 small
celery	1 stick	1 stick	1 stick
leek	1	1	1
turnip	1	1	1
onion	2 medium	2 medium	2 medium
dried mushrooms	2 heads	2 heads	2 heads
carrots	2	2	2
peppercorns	3	3	3
bayleaf	1	1	1
lemon	1	1	1
cloves	2	2	2
bread	1 crust	1 crust	1 crust
vinegar	$3\frac{1}{2}$ tb	3 tb	3 tb
ale	2pt	2pt	1l
butter	$2\frac{1}{2}$ tb	1oz	30g

	USA	Imperial	Metric
flour	$1\frac{1}{4}$ tb	*1 tb*	*1 tb*
sugar	$2\frac{1}{2}$ tsp	*2 tsp*	*2 tsp*
red wine	*1 cup*	*8 fl oz*	*2dl*
raisins	$\frac{1}{2}$ cup	*3oz*	*90g*
marinaded cherry	*15*	*15*	*15*
(see p 220)			

NOTE: Also suitable for bream and perch.

Prepare the carp by removing head, gills and scales with a sharp knife. Cut into pieces and rub with salt. Meanwhile cook celery, onion, turnip, leek, carrots and dried mushroom in the ale with peppercorns, bayleaf and cloves. Allow to boil for 15 min. Into a large pan place the pieces of carp, laying its head at the bottom of the pan to add flavour. Squeeze the lemon, keeping the juice. Put in chopped lemon rind and a crust of bread. Over the fish pour the strained ale in which the vegetables were boiled and cook rapidly for 25min, seeing that the fish does not burn. When ready, drain off the liquid to make *sauce*: brown 1 tb flour in butter, add 1 tsp of caramelised sugar and dilute with stock in which the carp has cooked. Add red wine, scalded raisins, lemon juice, more sugar to taste and marinaded cherries. Bring up to the boil 3 times, but make sure there is plenty of sauce, adding water if necessary. Serve the carp covered in sauce, decorated with raisins and slivers of lemon.

Fish solyanka baked

	USA	Imperial	Metric
fillets of white-fleshed fish	*2lb*	*2lb*	*1kg*
cabbage or sauerkraut	*2lb*	*2lb*	*1kg*
salt	*to taste*	*to taste*	*to taste*
butter	$2\frac{1}{2}$ tb	*1oz*	*30g*
breadcrumbs	$\frac{1}{2}$ cup	$\frac{1}{2}$oz	*15g*
tomato purée	$1\frac{1}{4}$ tb	*1 tb*	*1 tb*
dill-pickled cucumbers	*2*	*2*	*2*

79

	USA	Imperial	Metric
capers	*2 tsp*	*2 tsp*	*2 tsp*
olives	*15 to garnish*	*15 to garnish*	*15 to garnish*
onions	*2 large*	*2 large*	*2 large*
bayleaf	*1*	*1*	*1*
marinaded fruit	*to garnish*	*to garnish*	*to garnish*
dried mushrooms	*6*	*6*	*6*
lard or cooking fat	*¼ cup*	*2oz*	*60g*
onion	*1*	*1*	*1*
sugar	*1¼ tb*	*1 tb*	*1 tb*
flour	*1¼ tb*	*1 tb*	*1 tb*
salt	*1 tsp*	*1 tsp*	*1 tsp*

NOTE: Any large white-fleshed fish may be used.

Braise the cabbage or sauerkraut for 40min with chopped onion and the chopped dried mushrooms in a very little water. Remove bones and skin from the fish fillets and use to make stock. Cut the fish into portions and place in a pan with salt, pepper, capers, cucumbers peeled and with seeds removed, tomato purée, chopped onion softened in butter, fish stock and bayleaf. Cover the pan and simmer for 20min. Then add flour rubbed into the same amount of butter. Carefully so as not to break the pieces of fish, add the flour to the liquid in the pan and boil for a couple of minutes to thicken.

Take a well buttered fireproof dish lined with breadcrumbs. Spread half the braised cabbage or sauerkraut evenly and lay the fish on top. Over this pour the contents of the pan. Cover the fish with a second layer of cabbage, sprinkle this with breadcrumbs and dot with butter. Put in a hot oven for 10min. Before serving decorate with stoned olives, slices of lemon, marinaded grapes or plums (see p 220).

Fish cutlets and tefteli

Fillets or left-overs of any large white-fleshed fish are suitable.

Put through a mincer (grinder), mix with half the amount of crumb of bread soaked in milk, with salt and a little softened butter, to make either:

Cutlets rolled in breadcrumbs and then fried on either side for 10min and served with vegetables, *or*:

Fish tefteli which are balls made of the fish mixture with a little chopped onion softened in butter. These are slightly browned, placed in a casserole, covered in tomato sauce and cooked in the oven for 15min. They are usually served with buckwheat (see p 170).

Telnoye of any white fish fillets, minced (ground) and stuffed

	USA	Imperial	Metric
fillets	*1lb*	*1lb*	*500g*
bread	*4oz*	*4oz*	*120g*
milk	*2½ tb*	*2 tb*	*2 tb*
butter	*5 tb*	*2oz*	*60g*
egg, hard-boiled	*1*	*1*	*1*
raw egg	*1 yolk*	*1 yolk*	*1 yolk*
onion	*1 medium*	*1 medium*	*1 medium*
parsley	*1 sprig*	*1 sprig*	*1 sprig*
mushrooms	*¼lb*	*4oz*	*120g*
breadcrumbs, as needed			
salt, pepper, to taste			

Remove skin and any bones from the fillets, mince finely and mix with the bread soaked in milk and squeezed dry. Add salt and pepper to taste, 1 tb of softened butter and mix thoroughly to form a firm mass. Place rounded tablespoonfuls of the mixture onto a dampened cloth and form into flat rounds. On the centre of half the rounds put a walnut of filling:

Filling Cook the mushrooms in a little boiling water, drain. Soften the chopped onion in butter and add the chopped mushrooms. Mix this with chopped hard-boiled egg and finely chopped parsley. Cover the filling with the remaining rounds of fish mixture. Press the edges together forming crescents.

Brush with beaten egg and coat with breadcrumbs. Fifteen minutes before serving fry in butter browning well on each side. They can also be fried in advance and placed in a hot oven for 10min before serving.

Crayfish steamed soufflé

Crayfish abound in Russian rivers and are extensively used as flavouring, as garnishes, boiled and eaten hot with a spicy wine sauce, or else cold with mayonnaise, like lobster. They are usually obtainable at a good fishmonger's and are also sold deep-frozen.

	USA	Imperial	Metric
crayfish	½*lb*	*8oz*	*240g*
white fish meat	½*lb*	*8oz*	*240g*
eggs	*2*	*2*	*2*
mushroom	¼*lb*	*4oz*	*120g*
butter, melted	*5 tb*	*2oz*	*60g*
salt, to taste			

Finely chop the shelled crayfish and fish meat. Mince (grind) or else pound and rub through a sieve. Add the butter, well beaten eggs, salt and blend thoroughly. Put the mixture into a buttered basin lined with mushrooms which have been cooked quickly in a little salted water and drained. Cover the basin firmly as for a steamed pudding.

Forty minutes before serving set the crayfish soufflé to steam in boiling water two-thirds up the side of the basin. Serve turned out into a hot dish, surrounded by buttered potatoes and accompanied by hollandaise sauce.

I have used frozen scampi most successfully when crayfish was unobtainable, but when using frozen fish make sure that it thaws thoroughly and is very well drained, otherwise too much liquid emerges in the cooking.

Egg and butter

	USA	Imperial	Metric
eggs, hard-boiled	2	2	2
butter	½ cup	4oz	120g
lemon juice	1 tsp	1 tsp	1 tsp
salt	½ tsp	½ tsp	½ tsp

Melt the butter and to it add the peeled, chopped hard-boiled eggs, salt and lemon juice.

White wine sauce

	USA	Imperial	Metric
onion	1 medium	1 medium	1 medium
parsley	2 sprigs	2 sprigs	2 sprigs
butter	2½ tb	1oz	30g
fish stock	1 cup	8 fl oz	2dl
flour	1¼ tb	1 tb	1 tb
white wine	2½ tb	2 tb	2 tb
lemon juice	1 tsp	1 tsp	1 tsp
egg	1 yolk	1 yolk	1 yolk
salt	½ tsp	½ tsp	½ tsp

Chop and soften the onion in half the butter. Stir in flour and dilute with fish stock or bouillon; add salt, chopped parsley, simmer for 10min. Remove from heat, strain. Whip in egg yolk beaten in a tablespoon of butter, wine and lemon juice. Blend.

Dill-pickle sauce

To an ordinary white sauce add 2 tb of white wine and 4 tb of dill-pickle liquid. Simmer for 10 min and just before serving add 1 tb of butter and a little pepper.

Sour cream sauce

	USA	Imperial	Metric
sour cream	2 cup	1pt	$\frac{1}{2}l$
flour	3 tb	1oz	30g
butter	2½ tb	1oz	30g
salt, pepper, to taste			

Make a roux of the flour and butter and to this add the sour cream heated to boiling point. Season with salt and pepper and strain.

Hollandaise sauce with mustard

Add 1 tb prepared mustard to a cupful of hollandaise sauce and stir.

Red sauce

	USA	Imperial	Metric
stock	1½ cup	12 fl oz	4dl
flour	3 tb	1oz	30g
butter	2 tb	1oz	30g
tomato purée	2 tb	2 tb	2 tb
sugar	1¼ tb	1 tb	15g

Make a red roux with flour and butter. Dissolve with some stock to form a smooth mixture, the consistency of thick cream. Brown the tomato purée in a pan, add the remaining stock, mix with the diluted roux and simmer very gently for 20min.

Before serving add caramelised sugar: ie place sugar in a frying pan, dampen with water and, stirring with a wooden spatula, allow it to turn a very dark brown. Double the amount of water, stir until diluted, remove from heat and strain.

4
Meat

In former days meat was the prerogative of the well-to-do, as the peasant owned little stock and meat bought on the market was a luxury item, used only on special occasions. That is why many traditional Russian recipes concentrate on boiled meat—which has already been used to make stock for soup—and minced (ground) meat for which the cheaper cuts of a carcase can be used. A comprehensive Russian cookery book offers a dozen different ways of dishing up boiled meat as well as a number of recipes for minced (ground) meat.

As with other courses it is the unusual combinations of flavours and methods of cooking that are most typical of Russian cuisine.

Boiled beef baked with cheese

	USA	Imperial	Metric
meat from stock (see p 37)	*2lb*	*2lb*	*1kg*
butter	*1¼tb*	*1 tb*	*1 tb*
flour	*1¼ tb*	*1 tb*	*1 tb*
onion or leek	*1*	*1*	*1*
sour cream	*1½ cup*	*¾pt*	*4dl*
egg yolks	*2*	*2*	*2*
grated cheese	*4 tb*	*1oz*	*30g*
stock	*1 cup*	*8 fl oz*	*2dl*
salt, pepper, to taste			

Fry the chopped onion or leek in butter, add flour and brown. Pour on the sour cream and stock; bring to the boil. Beat up the egg yolks and add, together with salt and pepper.

Cut the boiled meat in pieces and put in a fireproof dish. Cover with the sauce and sprinkle the surface with grated cheese. Brown in a hot oven.

Boiled beef and marinaded mushrooms

	USA	Imperial	Metric
boiled beef	*1½lb*	*1½lb*	*750g*
vegetable oil	*2½ tb*	*2 tb*	*2 tb*
onion	*3 medium*	*3 medium*	*3 medium*
flour	*2½ tb*	*2 tb*	*2 tb*
mushrooms, marinaded (see p 223)	*¼lb*	*4oz*	*120g*
or button mushrooms	*1 tin*	*1 tin*	*1 tin*

87

	USA	Imperial	Metric
egg yolks	*3*	*3*	*3*
grated cheese	*1 cup*	*4oz*	*120g*
cream, sour or double (heavy)	*½ cup*	*4 fl oz*	*1dl*
salt, pepper, to taste			

NOTE: If no marinaded mushrooms are available, take a tin of button mushrooms, drain and let them stand in dill-pickle solution for several hours.

Slice the meat thinly and sprinkle each slice with grated cheese. Place these one on top of the other in a casserole.

Prepare the following sauce: fry the chopped onions in oil with the flour, stirring so that they should not burn. Add cream diluted with half the amount of water. Stir well and cook for a couple of minutes before adding chopped mushrooms and three well beaten yolks. Season. Heat through without boiling, pour over the meat and set in a medium oven for 15min.

Hussar's bake (steak with herring)

	USA	Imperial	Metric
steak, cut thick	*1½lb*	*1½lb*	*750g*
herring, fresh	*1 small*	*1 small*	*1 small*
egg	*1*	*1*	*1*
crustless bread (stale)	*3 slices*	*3 slices*	*3 slices*
spring onion	*1 medium*	*1 medium*	*1 medium*
carrots	*2*	*2*	*2*
vegetable oil	*2½ tb*	*2 tb*	*2 tb*
salt, to taste			

Sprinkle the surface of the meat with salt and leave for 30min. Chop onion and carrots and fry in a pan with hot oil. Brown the meat on all sides and make 5 or 6 deep incisions on one side without cutting it right through. Into these put the filling:
Filling Carefully fillet the herring removing all bones and skin, chop very finely. Add the crumb of stale bread, a little pepper, chopped spring onion and the egg. Mix thoroughly, adding 1 tsp of oil.

When the meat is stuffed, tie firmly with a thread to close the incisions. Place in a casserole on top of the vegetables with enough water or stock to cover the vegetables. Put the lid on firmly and braise gently for 45min, adding a little water if necessary to prevent burning.

Fillet of beef in wine

	USA	Imperial	Metric
fillet steak	1½lb	1½lb	750g
vegetable oil	1¼ tb	1 tb	1 tb
vinegar	2½ tsp	2 tsp	2 tsp
lard	5 tb	2oz	60g
red wine	1 wineglass	1 wineglass	1 wineglass
sugar	2 lumps	2 lumps	2 lumps
stock	5 tb	4 tb	4 tb
flour	1¼ tb	1 tb	1 tb

The meat should be browned on a spit, but can be browned on a hot frying pan without fat, basted with mixed oil and vinegar. Separately brown the sugar, add flour and mix with the meat gravy. Add wine and stock. Slice the meat and put in a small casserole, brushing each piece with lard or butter. Cover with the sauce and braise until tender—20 or 30min.

Serve each portion on a thick slice of crustless bread, fried on one side only, and accompanied by tomato salad.

Braised beef with horseradish

	USA	Imperial	Metric
rump steak	2lb	2lb	1kg
carrot	1	1	1
turnip	1	1	1
leek	1	1	1
celery	1 stick	1 stick	1 stick
onion	1	1	1
bayleaf	1	1	1

89

cloves	3	3	3
peppercorns	10	10	10
grated horseradish	8 tb	6 tb	6 tb
butter	½ cup	4oz	120g
wine (red or white)	1 cup	8 fl oz	2dl
streaky bacon	2 rashers	2 rashers	2 rashers
vinegar	2½ tsp	2 tsp	2 tsp
salt, to taste			

Brown the meat on all sides in a little butter. Place in a pan just large enough to hold the meat and the chopped vegetables, bacon cut in small pieces, bayleaf, cloves, peppercorns, salt. Sprinkle the meat with vinegar, pour on wine and equivalent amount of stock or water. Cover tightly with a lid and braise in a low oven for 1½–2hr.

Beef Stroganov with mustard

This is among the best known Russian recipes, created during the last century by the chef of Count Stroganov, who gave the dish its name. One of the prerequisites for success is that ingredients should not be too cold and also that both meat and sauce should be allowed to stand for several hours after being prepared.

	USA	Imperial	Metric
fillet of beef	2lb	2lb	1kg
onion	1 large	1 large	1 large
butter	5 tb	2oz	60g
sour cream	5 tb	4 tb	4 tb
mustard, prepared	½ tsp	½ tsp	½ tsp
tomato purée	1¼ tb	1 tb	1 tb
hot stock	1pt	1pt	½l
salt, pepper, to taste			

Prepare the meat at least two hours beforehand. First cut the fillet into slices, then into thin strips. Sprinkle with salt and pepper and allow to stand. If the meat is cut too thin it hardens in cooking. At the same time brown the flour in butter, work to a paste gradually adding the stock, tomato purée and mustard. Bring to the boil and strain. Allow to stand.

Twenty minutes before serving chop the onion finely and fry rapidly in butter with the meat, turning with a spatula, for 5 min and cooking only enough at a time to cover the bottom of the frying pan.

When the meat is ready, add sour cream to the sauce and place in a firmly lidded pan together with the meat and onion. Stand on an asbestos sheet on low heat for 10min to keep warm ('stand on the side of the stove', says the original recipe). Bring to near boiling just before serving.

The sauce can also be prepared omitting the mustard if preferred, while another variation adds thinly sliced mushrooms to the onions which are then fried separately from the meat.

Hunter's lunch

	USA	Imperial	Metric
rump steak	1lb	1lb	500g
ham	¼lb	4oz	120g
eggs	4	4	4
lard	¼lb	4oz	120g
spring onion	2	2	2
butter	1¼ tb	1 tb	1 tb
salt, pepper, to taste			

Make an omelette with the eggs, butter and chopped ham.

With a wooden mallet beat the rump into a flat pancake, sprinkle with salt and pepper. Lay the cooked omelette onto the flattened meat and roll firmly. Lard with strips of fat and bake in a hot oven for 20min. Carve into slices and serve with a sharp sauce. It is excellent cold and a good picnic dish.

Spiced sirloin (serves 8)

	USA	Imperial	Metric
joint of beef	*3–4lb*	*3–4lb*	*1½–2kg*
vinegar and water	*to cover*	*to cover*	*to cover*
mixed spice	*1 tb*	*1 tb*	*1 tb*
lard (fat)	*½lb*	*8oz*	*240g*
cloves	*3*	*3*	*3*
capers	*1¼ tb*	*1 tb*	*1 tb*
mushroom essence	*1 tsp*	*1 tsp*	*1 tsp*
wine (red or white)	*4 tb*	*3 tb*	*3 tb*
lemon	*½*	*½*	*½*
butter	*1¼ tb*	*1 tb*	*1 tb*
flour	*1¼ tb*	*1 tb*	*1 tb*
salt, pepper, to taste			

Soak the piece of meat in vinegar halved with water for 24hr with the mixed spice added to the liquid.

Lard the meat in a number of places with fat pounded with salt, pepper and cloves. Roast in hot oven for 1½hr, basting frequently with its own juice.

Brown flour in butter, dilute with a little stock or water, add wine, capers, mushroom essence, sliced lemon and bring to boil. Add gravy from the meat, strain and serve with the joint.

Zrazy à la Nelson

	USA	Imperial	Metric
beef (rump or fillet)	*1½lb*	*1½lb*	*750g*
mushrooms	*¼lb*	*4oz*	*120g*
onion	*2*	*2*	*2*
butter	*2½ tb*	*1oz*	*30g*
lard	*¼lb*	*4oz*	*120g*
bread, soft crumb	*3 tb*	*½oz*	*15g*
egg	*1*	*1*	*1*
salt, pepper, to taste			

Flatten the meat to the thickness of a little finger. Make criss-cross incisions and rub with beaten egg.

Fry the mushrooms, slice finely and mix with chopped lard. Chop the onions and soften in butter. Mix all together with bread rubbed to crumbs, salt and pepper. Lay the mixture on the flattened meat, roll firmly, place in a pan with butter and braise 30 or 40min. Cut into 8 pieces and serve with the strained gravy from the pan.

Klops

	USA	Imperial	Metric
rump steak	*1½lb*	*1½lb*	*750g*
onion	*2 medium*	*2 medium*	*2 medium*
rye bread (stale), crumb	*1 cup*	*4oz*	*120g*
flour	*1¼ tb*	*1 tb*	*1 tb*
butter	*2½ tb*	*2 tb*	*2 tb*
sour cream	*½ cup*	*4 fl oz*	*1dl*
bayleaf	*1*	*1*	*1*
salt, pepper, to taste			

Cut the meat into 8 pieces and with a wooden mallet flatten as thinly as possible. Salt slightly and dip in flour. Butter the bottom of a pan, put in bayleaf, pepper and the slices of meat. Sprinkle each with chopped onion and grated rye bread. Add 4 tb water and braise for 30min, shaking the pan so that the meat does not burn, adding a little water if necessary. Before serving put sour cream in the pan, heat through and serve with the meat.

Golubtsy (minced [ground] beef in cabbage leaves)

	USA	Imperial	Metric
minced (ground) meat	*1lb*	*1lb*	*500g*
cabbage	*½ head*	*½ head*	*½ head*
rice or barley	*1 cup*	*8oz*	*240g*
onion	*1 medium*	*1 medium*	*1 medium*
flour	*1¼ tb*	*1 tb*	*1 tb*
tomato purée	*2½ tb*	*2 tb*	*2 tb*

	USA	Imperial	Metric
sour cream	2½ tb	2 tb	2 tb
butter	2½ tb	2 tb	2 tb
salt, pepper, to taste			
parsley, to garnish			

NOTE: Veal can be used instead of beef.

Cook the rice or barley and allow to cool. Mix with the finely minced (ground) meat, add chopped onion softened in butter, also salt and pepper.

Take whole leaves of the cabbage and soften in boiling water for a good 5min. Drain well and allow to cool. Remove thick stalks to where the leaf proper begins, lay flat and put 1 tb of meat and rice filling on each. Roll up into small rolls, tie with thread, brown rapidly in butter and then lay in a casserole. Into the frying pan put tomato purée, sour cream, flour, salt, pepper and a little water. Bring to the boil and pour over the golubtsy in the casserole. Simmer with lid on for 30min on very low heat or else without a lid in a fairly hot oven. Serve in their own gravy and sprinkled with chopped parsley.

Bitki

These meat balls are a favourite Russian recipe and are different from hamburgers in that they are smaller, softer and juicier. This is due to the addition of bread soaked in milk, which absorbs the meat juices during cooking so that no gravy is produced by the meat balls. They can be made from beef alone, although I always prefer to use half beef and half veal or pork, which the butcher puts through the mincer (grinder) together with the selected piece of beef. The addition of chopped, softened onion is optional, though personally I always use it, as well as an egg yolk for binding.

	USA	Imperial	Metric
minced (ground) meat	1 lb	1 lb	500g
stale crumb	2 cup	5 oz	150g

	USA	Imperial	Metric
flour	6 tb	2oz	60g
milk	5 tb	4 tb	4 tb
butter or oil	5 tb	4 tb	4 tb
egg yolk (optional)	1	1	1
onion (optional)	1 medium	1 medium	1 medium
salt, pepper, to taste			

NOTE: Veal can be used instead of beef.

Soak the bread in milk, squeeze dry and mix with the minced meat. Add salt, pepper, chopped fried onion and egg yolk if desired. Mix thoroughly. Make approximately 16 meat balls, roll in flour put in pan, flatten slightly and fry in oil or butter, 5–7min on each side. Serve with sour cream sauce (see p 84) and mashed potato.

Tefteli (braised meat balls)

	USA	Imperial	Metric
minced (ground) beef	1lb	1lb	500g
onion	1 medium	1 medium	1 medium
stale crumb	2 cup	5oz	150g
flour	5 tb	4 tb	4 tb
butter or oil	2½ tb	2 tb	2 tb
meat stock	1 cup	½pt	¼l
tomato purée	2½ tb	2 tb	2 tb
bayleaf	½	½	½
garlic	1 clove	1 clove	1 clove
peppercorns	4	4	4
salt, pepper, to taste			

NOTE: Veal can be used instead of beef.

Prepare the meat as for bitki (see previous recipe), make 20 or 24 small balls, roll in flour and brown quickly in butter. Place in a small casserole, add meat stock, tomato purée, bayleaf, peppercorns and the clove of garlic crushed in salt. Cover the casserole firmly and braise on low heat or in a medium oven for 20min. Serve with buckwheat (see p 170), rice or potato purée.

Roast veal and caviar sauce (serves 8)

	USA	Imperial	Metric
leg of veal	3–4lb	3–4lb	1½–2kg
fat for larding	¼lb	4oz	120g
ham	½lb	8oz	240g
onion	1	1	1
leek	1	1	1
celery	½ stick	½ stick	½ stick
parsley	1 sprig	1 sprig	1 sprig
white wine	8 tb	6 fl oz	2dl
peppercorns	10	10	10
lemon rind	½ lemon	½ lemon	½ lemon
lemon juice	½ tb	½ tb	½ tb
butter	1¼ tb	1 tb	1 tb
stock	to cover	to cover	to cover
caviar	2½ tb	2 tb	2 tb
salt, to taste			

Lard the veal in a number of places with alternate thin strips of lean ham and fat. Into a large casserole put a layer of chopped vegetables, lay the veal on top and cover with wine and stock. Add peppercorns, grated lemon rind, salt, and cook in a fairly hot oven until the meat is soft (1½–2hr).

With stock from the cooking prepare the sauce: skim off any fat, strain the stock and add caviar to 1 cup stock, stirring until blended. Add butter and lemon juice, heat until butter is melted and serve over the sliced veal.

Roast veal with cherries

	USA	Imperial	Metric
veal joint	3lb	3lb	1½kg
cherries	½lb	½lb	500g
cinnamon	½ tsp	½ tsp	½ tsp
Madeira	½ cup	4 fl oz	1dl
cherry syrup	½ cup	4 fl oz	1dl
butter	2½ tb	2 tb	2 tb
flour	1¼ tb	1 tb	1 tb
salt, to taste			

Slightly salt the joint and make 20 or 30 deep incisions. Put 1 or 2 stoned cherries in each. Brush the joint with butter, sprinkle with cinnamon and place in a hot oven to brown.

Transfer the joint to a casserole, brush again with butter and sprinkle with flour. Cover with a lid and cook for 30–40min in a hot oven, then add Madeira, cherry syrup and butter. Replace the lid and continue cooking for a further 30min, basting frequently. Serve with its own sauce, adding a little stock if necessary.

Gourmet's cutlets

	USA	Imperial	Metric
veal chops	*8*	*8*	*8*
stewing beef	*1lb*	*1lb*	*½kg*
butter	*½ cup*	*4oz*	*120g*
cornflour (cornstarch)	*1½ tb*	*1 tb*	*1 tb*
cream	*2½ tb*	*2 tb*	*2 tb*
salt, pepper, to taste			

Cut the beef into slices, flatten with a wooden mallet, sprinkle with salt and pepper. Trim the veal chops, removing surplus bone and wrap each one in the flattened beef, tying with a thread. Place in a tightly lidded dish with melted butter and cook in a fairly hot oven for 30 or 40min, turning halfway through the cooking. When cooked, thicken the juice in the pan with cornflour, add cream and serve over the veal chops after discarding the beef.

Calves' liver cooked whole

	USA	Imperial	Metric
calves' liver	*1½lb*	*1½lb*	*750g*
lard	*½lb*	*8oz*	*240g*
carrot	*2 small*	*2 small*	*2 small*
leek	*½*	*½*	*½*
onion	*1 small*	*1 small*	*1 small*

	USA	Imperial	Metric
flour	½ tb	½ tb	½ tb
bayleaf	1	1	1
peppercorns	10	10	10
cloves	3	3	3
butter	2 tb	1½ tb	1½ tb
sour cream	½ cup	4oz	1dl
juniper berries (optional)	1 tb	1 tb	1 tb
stock	2 cup	¾pt	½l
milk	2 cup	¾pt	½l
salt, to taste			

Soak the liver in milk (or milk and water) for 2hr. Drain, remove membrane and lard it all over. Brown quickly in a frying pan. Put chopped vegetables and remaining lard chopped in pieces into a casserole with the spices and butter. Lay the liver on the vegetables. Add stock, sour cream, salt and flour; braise for 40min. Strain the sauce and pour over the sliced liver.

Breast of veal with raisins (serves 6)

	USA	Imperial	Metric
breast or shoulder of veal	3lb	3lb	1½kg
celery	1 stick	1 stick	1 stick
leek	½	½	½
carrot	1 medium	1 medium	1 meduim
parsley	2 sprigs	2 sprigs	2 sprigs
peppercorns	5	5	5
butter	2½ tb	2 tb	2 tb
flour	5 tb	4 tb	4 tb
bayleaf	1	1	1
raisins, seedless	½ cup	3oz	100g
stock	2 cup	1pt	¼l
white wine	½ cup	4 fl oz	1dl
lemon	½	½	½
sugar	2 lumps	2 lumps	2 lumps
salt, to taste			

NOTE: Can be prepared with breast of lamb.

Choose a breast which is not too fat or else meat from the shoulder, and cut into portions of 2 ribs each. Put the breast of veal into cold water to cover and bring to the boil. Skim and strain the stock, rinse the meat in cold water and return to the stock. Simmer for 30min with all the vegetables and condiments, when the meat should be soft.

Brown the flour in butter, dissolve in a little stock and bring up to the boil two or three times, adding the remaining stock. Put in raisins, slices of lemon with pips removed, sugar and wine. Return the veal to the sauce and bring to the boil again before serving.

Sweetbreads with crayfish

	USA	Imperial	Metric
sweetbreads	*2lb*	*2lb*	*1kg*
lard	*¼lb*	*4oz*	*120g*
butter	*2½ tb*	*1oz*	*30g*
onion, grated	*1*	*1*	*1*
crayfish, chopped	*1 cup*	*8oz*	*240g*
cheese, grated	*1 cup*	*4oz*	*120g*
flour	*½ tb*	*½ tb*	*½ tb*
stock	*1 cup*	*8 fl oz*	*2dl*
cream	*1 cup*	*8 fl oz*	*2dl*
nutmeg	*½ tsp*	*½ tsp*	*½ tsp*
salt, pepper, to taste			

NOTE: The crayfish can, if desired, be replaced by mushrooms.

Soak the sweetbreads in cold water for 2hr, drain and drop into salted boiling water to cook for 15min. Drain again and stand in cold water to harden. Remove any veins and lard with thinly sliced fat. Melt butter in a pan, add grated onion and flour stirring well to brown. Dilute with the stock and add grated cheese, salt, pepper and nutmeg. Stir well and when the cheese is melted put in cream and finally the sweetbreads. Cover the pan and simmer for 20min or until sweetbreads are soft. Before serving add cooked chopped crayfish to the gravy and heat through.

Shashlyk

This dish is not simply pieces of lamb barbecued on a spit. Essential to the preparation of shashlyk is the marinading of the meat for several hours—or overnight if a large piece of meat for 10 or 12 people is being used. While roasting, the meat should be frequently basted with the marinade and herbs can be thrown on the charcoal to add perfume and flavour.

	USA	Imperial	Metric
piece of lamb	*2–3lb*	*2–3lb*	*1–1½kg*
lamb kidneys	*4*	*4*	*4*
garlic	*2 cloves*	*2 cloves*	*2 cloves*
tomatoes	*1lb*	*1lb*	*½kg*
onion	*2*	*2*	*2*
parsley	*small bunch*	*small bunch*	*small bunch*
vinegar	*1¼pt*	*1pt*	*½l*
water	*1¼pt*	*1pt*	*½l*
pickling spice	*2½ tsp*	*2 tsp*	*2 tsp*
salt, pepper, to taste			

NOTE: Cossack friends of mine always add 8 or 10 tb brandy to the marinade, pouring it over the meat before adding the rest of the liquid.

Salt the meat all over and then lard with slivers of garlic. Place in an earthernware bowl, pour on the brandy if used, chop onion and parsley and sprinkle over the meat. Meanwhile boil the water, vinegar and spices together and allow to cool. Pour on the meat so that it is well covered. If not, either turn frequently or else increase the marinading liquid in same proportion. Cover with a cloth and stand in a cool place for several hours.

Before using, remove the meat from the marinade, cut into small portions and thread onto spits alternately with quarters of kidney and whole tomatoes.

Cook over hot charcoal, basting with the marinade. If no barbecue can be arranged the meat can be cooked on a hot iron pan or under a grill at high temperature, so that the meat browns quickly and even slightly scorches on the surface.

Serve with rice, spring onion and quarters of lemon.

Breast of lamb with caraway sauce

	USA	Imperial	Metric
breast of lamb	2lb	2lb	1kg
carrot	1	1	1
celery	1 stick	1 stick	1 stick
leek	$\frac{1}{2}$	$\frac{1}{2}$	$\frac{1}{2}$
onion	2	2	2
Caraway sauce			
butter	$1\frac{1}{4}$ tb	1 tb	1 tb
flour	$1\frac{1}{4}$ tb	1 tb	1 tb
caraway seed	$1\frac{1}{4}$ tb	1 tb	1 tb
sugar	$1\frac{1}{4}$ tb	1 tb	1 tb
vinegar	$2\frac{1}{2}$ tb	2 tb	2 tb
stock	1 cup	8 fl oz	2dl
salt, pepper, to taste			

Simmer the breast of lamb until soft with the chopped vege-tables and water barely to cover.

For the sauce: brown the flour in butter, stirring constantly, dilute with the stock in which the lamb was cooked, add caraway seed, sugar, vinegar and bring to the boil. When it thickens serve with the lamb.

Lamb to taste like venison (serves 10 or 15)

	USA	Imperial	Metric
hind quarter of a lamb	*8–10lb*	*8–10lb*	*4–5kg*
fat or lard	*1 cup*	*8oz*	*240g*
vinegar	*½pt*	*½pt*	*¼l*
ale	*½pt*	*½pt*	*¼l*
peppercorns	*10*	*10*	*10*
bayleaf	*2*	*2*	*2*
juniper berries	*7½ tb*	*6 tb*	*6 tb*
butter	*2½ tb*	*2 tb*	*2 tb*
sour cream	*10 tb*	*8 tb*	*8 tb*

Hang the fresh meat in a cool place for two days, then remove skin and fat and marinade for another two days in ale and vinegar brought to the boil with spices and equal amounts of water and cooled. The meat to be turned several times during the period. Rinse the meat; lard with fat and roast in the oven, reckoning the time according to the weight of the joint and basting it with butter. Just before taking out of the oven pour the sour cream over the joint. As soon as this turns a deep yellow take out the meat and carve, then serve with its own gravy.

Roast Lamb

Roast lamb in Russia, is not accompanied by mint sauce. It is, in fact, usually served with a sauce of sour cream or wine or onion, and accompanied by buckwheat (see p 170) or rice. The next two recipes are useful for dealing with left-overs from the joint.

Lamb and apple ragout

	USA	Imperial	Metric
cold meat	*1lb*	*1lb*	*500g*
onions	*2*	*2*	*2*
oil	*1¼ tb*	*1 tb*	*1 tb*
flour	*1¼ tb*	*1 tb*	*1 tb*
garlic	*1 clove*	*1 clove*	*1 clove*
cooking apples	*2*	*2*	*2*
salt, to taste			

Cut the left-over meat into small pieces and season. Fry the chopped onion in oil with crushed clove of garlic and mix in the flour, diluting with a cupful of water. Add chopped apples and bring to the boil before putting in the meat. Simmer till apple and onion are quite soft.

Lamb and rice bake

	USA	Imperial	Metric
cold meat	*1lb*	*1lb*	*500g*
rice	*1 cup*	*6oz*	*175g*
butter	*½ tb*	*½ tb*	*½ tb*
parsley	*6 sprigs*	*6 sprigs*	*6 sprigs*
spring onion	*1 bunch*	*1 bunch*	*1 bunch*
lemon	*1*	*1*	*1*
salt, pepper, to taste			

Cook the rice in a pan with butter and water (2 fingers above the surface of the rice). When nearly ready (15min) add the left-over meat cut into pieces, salt, pepper, mix and transfer to a buttered dish. Finish baking in a medium oven until rice is soft. Serve with chopped spring onion, sprinkled with parsley and with quarters of lemon.

Braised pork with prune sauce

	USA	Imperial	Metric
pork	2lb	2lb	1kg
wine (white)	½ cup	¼pt	1dl
vinegar	10 tb	8 tb	8 tb
juniper berries	5 tb	4 tb	4 tb
peppercorns	6	6	6
oil	1¼ tb	1 tb	1 tb
sugar	2½ tb	2 tb	2 tb
cinnamon	½ tsp	½ tsp	½ tsp
bayleaf	1	1	1
crumb of stale bread	5 tb	4 tb	4 tb
prunes, or tinned prune purée	½lb	8oz	240g
salt, to taste			

Remove skin and superfluous fat from pork. Put in a casserole with wine and vinegar mixed with an equal quantity of water, salt, pepper, bayleaf and juniper berries. Braise in a covered casserole for 1½hr, frequently turning the meat.

Prune sauce Cook prunes in a little water and rub through a sieve. Fry the breadcrumbs in butter, add prune purée, sugar and cinnamon. Dilute to required thickness with strained liquid from the casserole. Serve with the pork and boiled potatoes.

Solyanka

	USA	Imperial	Metric
assorted cold meats	1lb	1lb	500g
sauerkraut	1lb	1lb	500g
dill-pickled cucumber	2	2	2
onion	2	2	2
tomato purée	4 tb	3 tb	3 tb
flour	1¼ tb	1 tb	1 tb
capers	1¼ tb	1 tb	1 tb
bayleaf	1	1	1
butter	5 tb	2oz	60g
breadcrumbs	4 tb	3 tb	3 tb

	USA	Imperial	Metric
vinegar	*1¼ tb*	*1 tb*	*1 tb*
sugar	*1 dsp*	*1 dsp*	*1 dsp*
meat stock	*1 cup*	*8 fl oz*	*2dl*
salt, pepper, to taste			

Drain the sauerkraut well and then chop. Place in a saucepan with a spoonful of butter and meat stock, leaving a few table-spoonfuls aside. Cover the pan and simmer for 40min.

Add one chopped fried onion, tomato purée, vinegar, salt, sugar, bayleaf and pepper. Simmer for another 10min.

Brown the remaining butter with flour and add, stirring, to the cabbage. Bring to the boil.

Cut the assorted meat into small pieces and fry with the second onion, sliced in rings. Add the cucumbers, sliced, capers and remaining meat stock. Cover and simmer for 5min.

Into a casserole place a layer of sauerkraut, then the meat and cucumbers, cover with another layer of sauerkraut, sprinkle with breadcrumbs, dot with butter and bake on the top shelf of a hot oven for 10 or 15 min.

Can be served with olives, cranberries, pickles.

Bear

In a cookery book published in Moscow in 1965 there is a curious note about bear meat. It has, they say, a peculiar though pleasant flavour. But it should be kept in a marinade for at least four days to soften and then, before finally roasting, it should be braised for 5–6hr in the marinade liquid diluted with the same amount of stock made from the bones.

SAUCES FOR MEAT

Onion and apple sauce (for roast or boiled meat)

	USA	Imperial	Metric
onions	2	2	2
flour	1¼ tb	1 tb	1 tb
butter	1 cup	8oz	240g
sugar	1¼ tb	1 tb	1 tb
lemon	1	1	1
apple juice or blackberry	1 cup	8 fl oz	2dl

Bake the onion, skin and cut into pieces. Make a roux of butter and flour, dissolve in 8 tb water, stock or gravy from the roast. Bring to boil and strain. Add lemon juice, sugar and fruit juice and heat until sugar is melted.

Herring sauce (for cold meat)

	USA	Imperial	Metric
olive oil	2½ tb	2 tb	2 tb
mustard	1 tsp	1 tsp	1 tsp
eggs, hard-boiled	3	3	3
herring, salted	½	½	½
onion	1	1	1
cream	½ cup	4 fl oz	1dl
vinegar	2 tsp	2 tsp	2 tsp
sugar	½ tb	½ tb	½ tb

Rub yolks of hard-boiled eggs with oil, mustard, sugar and grated or very finely-chopped onion. Remove skin and all bones from the herring, cut into small pieces and mix with the sauce. Add cream and vinegar. Stir well.

Beetroot (beet) sauce (for roast or braised meat and poultry)

	USA	Imperial	Metric
beetroot (beet)	½lb	8oz	240g
sugar	1¼ tb	1 tb	1 tb
butter	2½ tb	2 tb	2 tb
egg white	1	1	1
lemon	½	½	½

Boil the beet in water until soft, skin and cut into pieces. Sieve or put through mincer. Add sugar and butter, simmer until all is blended. Chill. Fold in white of egg stiffly beaten, the juice and grated rind of half a lemon. Stir well and serve.

Mushroom and sherry sauce

	USA	Imperial	Metric
mushrooms	6 large	6 large	6 large
butter	1¼ tb	1 tb	1 tb
flour	1¼ tb	1 tb	1 tb
sherry	5 tb	4 tb	4 tb
lemon	¼	¼	¼
cream	2½ tb	2 tb	2 tb
chicken stock (cube)	1 cup	8 fl oz	2dl
salt, pepper, to taste			

Melt half the butter in a pan with lemon juuce and half the stock. Put in the mushrooms, bring to the boil. Remove the mushrooms with a perforated spoon, slice and return to sauce. Brown the flour in butter, dissolve with remaining stock and strain. Stir in the sherry and add to the mushroom sauce. Bring to the boil once, stir in the cream and heat through without boiling.

Madeira sauce with saffron

	USA	Imperial	Metric
butter	½ tb	½ tb	½ tb
flour	1¼ tb	1 tb	1 tb

	USA	Imperial	Metric
stock	*2 cup*	*1pt*	*4dl*
cayenne pepper	*1 pinch*	*1 pinch*	*1 pinch*
saffron	*1 pinch*	*1 pinch*	*1 pinch*
Madeira	*1 wineglass*	*1 wineglass*	*1 wineglass*

Prepare a white sauce with flour, butter and stock to which is added the pinch of cayenne pepper and salt to taste. Bring the Madeira to the boil with a pinch of saffron. Cool, strain and add to the suace. Heat through before serving.

Red wine sauce

	USA	Imperial	Metric
butter	*1¼ tb*	*1 tb*	*1 tb*
flour	*1¼ tb*	*1 tb*	*1 tb*
lemon	*¼*	*¼*	*¼*
red wine	*½ cup*	*4 fl oz*	*1dl*
sugar	*2 tsp*	*2 tsp*	*2 tsp*
egg yolks	*2*	*2*	*2*
stock (or water)	*1 cup*	*8 fl oz*	*2dl*

Brown the flour in butter and dissolve in stock or water. Add lemon juice, wine and sugar. Bring to the boil and strain. Just before serving whip in the egg yolks and heat through.

5

Poultry and Game

Poussin roasted in bechamel

	USA	Imperial	Metric
poussins	2	2	2
For sauce:			
butter	2½ tb	2 tb	2 tb
milk or cream	1½ cup	12 fl oz	3dl
flour	1 cup	4oz	120g
nutmeg	pinch	pinch	pinch
salt, to taste			

The poussins (or very small chickens) can be roasted either on a spit or in the oven. Meanwhile prepare the sauce given below. When ready coat the birds all over with the sauce and return to the oven for the sauce to brown. Cut each bird in half. Mix the remaining bechamel with gravy from the roasting pan and pour over each portion.

Bechamel sauce With the flour and butter make a white roux. Dissolve in milk or cream and season with salt and nutmeg. Simmer, stirring, till thick.

Poussin casseroled with green peas

	USA	Imperial	Metric
poussins	2	2	2
shelled peas	2 cup	1lb	500g
sugar	2½ tsp	2 tsp	2 tsp
flour	1¼ tb	1 tb	1 tb
cream	1 cup	8 fl oz	2dl
egg	1	1	1
butter	4 tb	3 tb	3 tb
breadcrumbs	½ cup	4 tb	4 tb
salt, to taste			

Cut the birds in half, dry, sprinkle with salt and put in a casserole barely covered with water. Add the peas, 1 tb melted butter and simmer for 30min. Take out the chicken and add sugar and flour to the casserole (chopped parsley is optional). Just before serving stir in the cream. Brush the chicken halves with beaten egg, coat well with breadcrumbs and fry in the remaining butter. Serve surrounded with peas and creamy gravy.

Roast chicken with sardine stuffing

	USA	Imperial	Metric
chicken	3½lb	3½lb	1¾kg
sardines	1 tin	1 tin	1 tin
milk	2½ tb	2 tb	2 tb
bread, crumb	¼ cup	2 tb	2 tb

	USA	Imperial	Metric
egg	*1*	*1*	*1*
grated cheese	*1¼ tb*	*1 tb*	*1 tb*
parsley, chopped	*1¼ tb*	*1 tb*	*1 tb*
salt, pepper, to taste			

Stuffing Mash the sardines with the oil from the tin; soak the bread in milk and squeeze out excess moisture; beat the egg and stir into the bread with the grated cheese and parsley. Add the mashed sardines and stuff the bird before roasting in the usual way.

BONING A CHICKEN

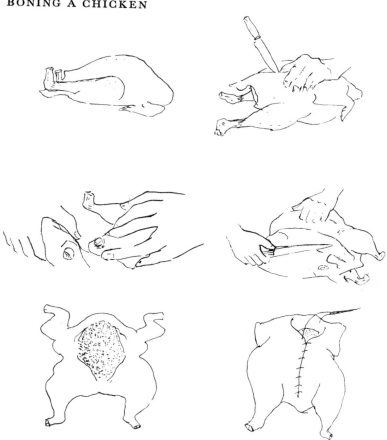

Boiled chicken stuffed with ham and rice (serves 6)

	USA	Imperial	Metric
chicken	4lb	4lb	2kg
rice	1½ cup	9oz	270g
ham, chopped	1 cup	6oz	180g
eggs	3	3	3
butter	1 cup	8oz	240g
nutmeg	1 pinch	1 pinch	1 pinch
salt, pepper, to taste			
Madeira sauce (see below)			

Boil the rice for 12min taking care not to overcook it. Drain, add butter, chopped ham, beaten eggs and nutmeg. Season. Mix well and cool. Bone the chicken and stuff with rice, stitching up the back to retain the stuffing. Put into boiling stock (see p 37 or chicken cube) to cover. Cook very gently for 2hr. Serve with Madeira sauce.

Madeira sauce

	USA	Imperial	Metric
flour	1¼ tb	1 tb	1 tb
butter	2½ tb	2 tb	2 tb
water	1 cup	8 fl oz	2dl
Madeira	1 wineglass	1 wineglass	1 wineglass
salt, a pinch			

Heat the butter and flour together to make a roux gradually adding the water, stirring constantly to make a creamy sauce. Season with a little salt. In a separate pan bring the Madeira to the boil and then blend with the sauce.

Chicken Kiev (serves 2)

	USA	Imperial	Metric
chicken breast	2	2	2
flour	1 cup	4oz	120g
butter	¼ cup	2oz	60g

	USA	Imperial	Metric
breadcrumbs	5 tb	4 tb	4 tb
egg	1	1	1
salt, pepper, to taste			

NOTE: Fresh chicken should be used for this dish because the flesh of frozen birds is apt to be too flaccid.

If a whole chicken is being used, carefully remove the breast from the carcase. Breast of chicken bought in 'portions' is quite suitable.

Put each breast on a wooden board and separate the little fillet from the main breast. Flatten both with a heavy cleaver as thinly as possible. Sprinkle with salt and pepper. Take butter, chilled hard in the refrigerator, and form into 2 small cylinders. Lay these on the chicken breasts, cover with the flattened fillet and roll the meat tightly round the butter. Dip in flour and return to the refrigerator for a couple of hours to harden.

Beat the egg ready for dipping, put breadcrumbs onto a plate and heat oil in the deep-fry pan until very hot but not smoking. Take the floured chicken breasts, dip in egg and coat with breadcrumbs, making sure they are well coated all over. Place in the basket and fry for 7 min, so that the flesh is cooked through and the butter inside just melted. Serve immediately with green peas.

Pozharsky cutlets (minced [ground] chicken rissoles)

	USA	Imperial	Metric
chicken	3½lb	3½lb	1¾kg
white crumb	1 cup	4oz	120g
milk	7½ tb	6 tb	6 tb
breadcrumbs	2½ tb	2 tb	2 tb
butter	1 cup	8oz	240g
egg	1	1	1
salt, pepper, to taste			

Remove flesh and skin from the chicken carcase and put both through the mincer twice over. Soak the crustless bread in milk, squeeze out excess liquid and mix with the minced (ground) chicken. Add salt, pepper and 1 tb of melted butter. Divide into oblong cutlets. Dip in beaten egg and coat thoroughly in breadcrumbs. Fry in hot butter for approximately 5min each side until the breadcrumbs are crusted and then cover the pan with a lid and leave on low heat for another 5min. Serve with mushroom sauce (see following recipe).

Dried mushroom sauce

	USA	Imperial	Metric
dried mushrooms	2 tb	1oz	30g
butter	1¼ tb	1 tb	1 tb
flour	2 tb	1½ tb	1½ tb
sour cream	½ cup	4 fl oz	1dl
salt, to taste			

Soak the dried mushrooms for 2hr. Drain, keeping the liquid, simmer in butter until soft and cut into small pieces. Brown the flour with the butter, dilute with mushroom liquid, stirring to remove any lumps. Season and add the mushroom pieces. Simmer for 15min and add sour cream just before serving.

Chicken bitki stuffed with mushrooms

	USA	Imperial	Metric
chicken	3½lb	3½lb	1¾kg
white crumb	½ cup	2oz	60g
milk	2½ tb	2 tb	2 tb
mushrooms	¼lb	4oz	120g
flour	1¼ tb	1 tb	1 tb
butter	2½ tb	2 tb	2 tb
breadcrumbs	2½ tb	2 tb	2 tb
egg	1	1	1
salt, pepper, to taste			

Prepare minced (ground) chicken as for cutlets (see p 113). Clean and slice the mushrooms and simmer for 15min in 1 tb butter. Add flour and simmer another 10min till the mixture thickens; season and cool. Shape the chicken into flat round patties and put a little mushroom filling in the centre of each. Join the edges of the minced chicken firmly round the filling, shaping into balls. Dip in beaten egg, coat with breadcrumbs and fry 5min each side in hot butter till the breadcrumbs form a crisp crust.

Chicken livers and sour cream

	USA	Imperial	Metric
chicken livers, chopped	2 cup	14oz	420g
butter	2½ tb	2 tb	2 tb
sour cream	½ cup	4 fl oz	1dl
flour	1¼ tb	1 tb	1 tb
parsley, chopped	1¼ tb	1 tb	1 tb
salt, pepper, to taste			

Scald the chicken livers in boiling water, rinse in cold water and fry rapidly in hot butter, browning them all over. Make a sour cream sauce (see p 84) with flour, butter and cream. Pour over the chicken livers in the pan, add chopped parsley and season. Simmer for 5min before serving.

Kournik (serves 6)

	USA	Imperial	Metric
chicken	3½lb	3½lb	1¾kg
onion	3 medium	3 medium	3 medium
celery	1 stick	1 stick	1 stick
peppercorns	8	8	8
cloves	3	3	3
bayleaf	1	1	1
mushrooms	½lb	½lb	240g
parsley, chopped	1½ tb	1 tb	1 tb
lemon juice	2 tsp	2 tsp	2 tsp
nutmeg, ground	pinch	pinch	pinch
cream	½ cup	4 fl oz	1dl

	USA	Imperial	Metric
butter	*5 tb*	*4 tb*	*4 tb*
rice	*1 cup*	*6oz*	*180g*
eggs, hard-boiled	*3*	*3*	*3*
dill weed, dried	*4 tb*	*3 tb*	*3 tb*
short crust pastry (see p 184)			
salt, pepper, to taste			

Steam the chicken in water half-way up, with neck and giblets cut into pieces, 3 whole onions, chopped celery, peppercorns, cloves and bayleaf until chicken is tender (1–1½hr).

Take out the chicken and strain the stock. Keep to one side. Chop the onions, drain well and fry in butter.

With some of the chicken stock boil the rice for 15min, until the stock (2 fingers above the level of the rice) is absorbed. Chop the hard-boiled eggs, mix with dill weed and stir into the rice with the onion. Season to taste.

Remove the flesh from the carcase of the chicken and cut into pieces. Slice and fry mushrooms in butter, mix with the chicken and stir in lemon juice, nutmeg, cream and a little stock. Well butter a fireproof dish and spread a layer of rice, cover with the chicken and mushroom and end with another layer of rice.

Roll out the pastry very thinly and cover the dish, pressing down the edges well and making 3 incisions along the top. Brush with milk and bake in a preheated fairly hot oven until the crust is browned.

Turkey fillets with cherry purée (serves 8)

	USA	Imperial	Metric
small turkey	*10lb*	*10lb*	*5kg*
Madeira	*4 tb*	*3 tb*	*3 tb*
butter	*1¼tb*	*1 tb*	*1 tb*
cherries	*1½lb*	*1½lb*	*700g*
cinnamon	*pinch*	*pinch*	*pinch*
nutmeg	*pinch*	*pinch*	*pinch*
cardamom seeds	*2*	*2*	*2*

	USA	Imperial	Metric
peppercorns	4	4	4
sugar	5 *tb*	4 *tb*	4 *tb*
salt, to taste			

Slice turkey breasts into portions, slightly flattening each piece. Salt each piece and sprinkle with Madeira. Leave for 15min. Melt butter in a pan and cook the turkey slices on low heat for 20min, browning each side.

Simmer the stoned cherries with cinnamon, nutmeg, cardamom, peppercorns and sugar until quite soft. Rub through a sieve and bring to the boil. Cover each slice of turkey with hot cherry purée and serve.

If only one side of the turkey breast is used (for 4 people) the bird can be subsequently roasted in the usual way, the empty breast being filled with stuffing held in place by the skin drawn up over it and stitched to the breast bone.

Roast turkey, duck or goose

These are roasted in the usual way but the stuffings vary considerably. Among the favourites are those made with calves' liver (see below), sauerkraut (see p 118) and buckwheat (see p 118).

Calves' liver stuffing

	USA	Imperial	Metric
calf liver	1lb	1lb	500g
stale crumb	2 cup	4oz	120g
milk	½ cup	4 fl oz	1dl
butter	4 tb	2 oz	60g
eggs, separated	2	2	2
sugar	1 tsp	1 tsp	1 tsp
breadcrumbs	2 tb	2 tb	2 tb
nutmeg	1 pinch	1 pinch	1 pinch
parsley	2 sprigs	2 sprigs	2 sprigs
salt, pepper, to taste			

Soak the bread in milk and squeeze out excess liquid. Remove membrane from liver, cut in pieces and pass through the mincer (grinder) together with the bread. Add egg yolks, butter, salt, pepper, nutmeg and chopped parsley. Mix well, gradually adding the breadcrumbs and finally stiffly-whipped egg whites.

Sauerkraut stuffing (used mainly for goose)

	USA	Imperial	Metric
sauerkraut	1lb	1lb	500g
butter	2 tb	1½ tb	1½ tb
onion	3 medium	3 medium	3 medium
caraway seed	½ heaped tb	½ heaped tb	½ heaped tb
salt, to taste			

Drain the sauerkraut of excess liquid and chop. Braise in a covered pan for 20min with chopped onion and butter. Cool. Before stuffing rub the inside of the bird with salt and caraway seed.

Buckwheat stuffing

	USA	Imperial	Metric
neck and giblets to make stock			
carrot	1	1	1
onion	1	1	1
leek	1	1	1
mushrooms, dried	1¼ tb	1 tb	1 tb
butter	1 tb	1 tb	1 tb
buckwheat	1½lb	1½lb	750g
egg	1	1	1
parsley	2 sprigs	2 sprigs	2 sprigs
salt, pepper, to taste			

With giblets, neck, carrot, onion, leek and mushrooms make a stock. Remove the mushrooms and chop. Strain the stock and replace the mushrooms, chopped parsley, salt and pepper in 2 cups of the stock.

Mix the buckwheat with beaten egg to coat the grains, then put into the stock and cook fast for 10min. Reduce heat and simmer until soft. Add more salt if necessary and cool before mixing with the mushrooms and stuffing the bird.

Ragout of leftovers from any roast bird

cold bird	USA	Imperial	Metric
stock	2 cup	$\frac{3}{4}pt$	4dl
butter	1 tb	1 tb	1 tb
flour	$\frac{1}{2}$ tb	$\frac{1}{2}$ tb	$\frac{1}{2}$ tb
apples	3	3	3
table wine	$\frac{1}{2}$ cup	4 fl oz	1dl
salt, pepper, to taste			

Remove all meat from the carcase and cut into pieces. Rub flour and butter in a casserole, dissolve with stock and add pieces of cold bird, peeled and thinly sliced apples, salt, pepper and wine. Bring to the boil then simmer for 10min, until the apples are soft.

Braised duck stuffed with noodles

	USA	Imperial	Metric
duck	1	1	1
noodles	$\frac{3}{4}lb$	$\frac{3}{4}lb$	350g
cloves	2	2	2
celery	1 stick	1 stick	1 stick
leek	$\frac{1}{2}$	$\frac{1}{2}$	$\frac{1}{2}$
onion	1	1	1
bayleaf	2	2	2
peppercorns	8	8	8
mushrooms	$\frac{1}{2}lb$	8oz	240g
butter	$2\frac{1}{2}$ tb	$1\frac{1}{2}$ tb	$1\frac{1}{2}$ tb
flour	5 tb	4 tb	4 tb
cream	$\frac{1}{2}$ cup	4 fl oz	1dl
egg yolks	2	2	2
salt, to taste			

Cut the duck down the back and carefully remove backbone. Rub the inside of the bird with salt and ground cloves. Boil the noodles in salted water and drain. Beat the yolks, add sliced mushroom, butter and salt. Mix with the noodles and stuff the duck. Stitch up the opening.

Put the duck in casserole just large enough to contain it and cover with mushroom stock (see p 38). Surround with chopped vegetables, peppercorns and bayleaf. Cook until soft for about 2hr in fairly hot oven. Make a thick sauce of butter, flour and strained stock to serve with the duck.

Hazel hen or grouse in sour cream

Simmer the required number of birds in a casserole with 6 tb of sour cream poured over each bird. The casserole should be firmly closed and left on very low heat for 1½–2hr depending on the size of the birds.

Blackcock or partridge with chestnuts

	USA	Imperial	Metric
blackcock	*2*	*2*	*2*
butter	*5 tb*	*2oz*	*60g*
stock	*1 cup*	*½pt*	*¼l*
sour cream	*½ cup*	*4 fl oz*	*1dl*
chestnuts	*2 cup*	*12oz*	*350g*
milk	*2 cup*	*¾pt*	*4dl*
salt, pepper, to taste			

Melt half the butter in a casserole and simmer the birds slowly for 20min, adding a little water to prevent burning. Add stock, sour cream, salt and pepper and continue braising in the covered casserole for 30min, until cooked.

Meanwhile scald and peel the chestnuts, boil in milk with the remainder of the butter until completely soft. Add to the casserole and continue braising for 5 or 10min.

Snipe or pigeon with lemon sauce

	USA	Imperial	Metric
snipe	*4*	*4*	*4*
lard	*½ cup*	*4oz*	*120g*
white crumb	*2 cup*	*4oz*	*120g*
egg	*2*	*2*	*2*
flour	*1¼ tb*	*1 tb*	*1 tb*
meat cube	*1*	*1*	*1*
lemon	*½*	*½*	*½*
butter	*1 cup*	*8oz*	*240g*
bread	*4 slices*	*4 slices*	*4 slices*
salt, pepper, to taste			

Roast the well larded birds in a medium oven. Meanwhile cut up giblets very finely, mix with crumb of white bread, 1 tb butter, 1 yolk and 1 whole egg. Add salt and pepper. Fry four slices (or 8 half slices) of bread in butter, spread each with the giblet mixture and put in the oven for 10min before serving.

Lemon sauce   Make a sauce of flour browned in butter, diluted with a cup of stock made with a meat cube. Add the juice of ½ lemon and bring to boiling point.

Serve each bird covered in lemon sauce with 2 half slices of garnished fried bread.

6

Vegetables and Vegetarian Dishes

Russians are not vegetable conscious. The usual accompaniment to the main dish is potato—boiled, mashed, roast or in chips as thin as 'straws'. Buckwheat or rice also serve as vegetables. Mushrooms, cucumbers fresh or salted and mixed salads or marinaded fruit come with the meat.

When boiled, a vegetable is generally disguised with some sauce, otherwise it is baked, stuffed or minced (ground) and made into 'cutlets', ie flattened oblong rissoles.

Breadcrumb sauce

Breadcrumb sauce is used for beans, cauliflower, cabbage, green peas or marrow. Brown 2 heaped tb of breadcrumbs in 3–4 tb of melted butter and pour over the vegetable.

Egg and wine sauce

> *3 egg yolks*
> *2 tb sugar*
> *1 wineglass white wine*
> *¼ large lemon, juice and peel*

Served with artichokes, asparagus, boiled potato.
Rub together the sugar and the egg yolks, add slices of lemon peel (without pith) and gradually stir in the wine. Stirring all the time stand in boiling water until the sauce thickens, without allowing it to boil. Remove the lemon peel and just before serving stir in the lemon juice.

Vegetables in sour cream

This is the most usual way of serving boiled vegetables and the preparation of each varies so slightly that it is sufficient to give a general indication. This applies to potatoes, beetroot (beet), turnip, squash or marrow, sweet corn, celery, carrots, string beans or mushrooms, which should first be scalded and fried.

Prepare the vegetables, slice if necessary, cook gently in 1 tb of melted butter and just enough water to cover. When cooked, remove from the pan, drain, salt and put back into a saucepan with 4–6 tb of sour cream. Bring to the boil and serve immediately.

Vegetables in sour cream, baked

Alternatively, place the cooked, drained vegetable in a buttered dish, salt, pour on the sour cream, sprinkle thickly with breadcrumbs or grated cheese, dot with butter and brown in a hot oven.

Potatoes in white wine

	USA	Imperial	Metric
potatoes	*8 medium*	*8 medium*	*8 medium*
butter	*1 tb*	*2oz*	*60g*
onion	*1*	*1*	*1*
parsley	*2 sprigs*	*2 sprigs*	*2 sprigs*
flour	*1¼ tb*	*1 tb*	*1 tb*
stock	*1 cup*	*8 fl oz*	*2dl*
white wine	*½ cup*	*4 fl oz*	*1 dl*
salt, pepper, to taste			

Boil the peeled potatoes. Fry the chopped onion and parsley with melted butter and flour. Cook for 2–3min and add stock and wine. Cut each potato in four and add to the sauce. Simmer until sauce thickens.

Potato galushky

	USA	Imperial	Metric
potatoes	*4 large*	*4 large*	*4 large*
butter	*2½ tb*	*2 tb*	*2 tb*
eggs	*2*	*2*	*2*
flour	*1¼ tb*	*1 tb*	*1 tb*
breadcrumbs	*1¼ tb*	*1 tb*	*1 tb*
salt, pepper, to taste			

Boil the potatoes in their skins, peel and mash while hot, adding flour, eggs, salt and pepper. Stir or beat until completely blended. Form into small round balls and drop these into boiling salted water. Cook for 15min without allowing the water to boil.

Drain well, put in a dish, pour on melted butter and sprinkle with fried breadcrumbs. Place in a hot oven for a few minutes.

Potato cutlets

	USA	Imperial	Metric
potatoes	*2lb*	*2lb*	*1kg*
egg yolks	*2*	*2*	*2*
flour	*½ cup*	*2oz*	*60g*
butter	*5 tb*	*4 tb*	*4 tb*
salt, pepper, to taste			

Peel the potatoes, cut in pieces and boil. Drain off the water, leaving the potatoes for a few minutes on very low heat to dry. Mash while hot, adding butter and egg yolks, salt and pepper. Make boat-shaped cutlets, coat in flour and fry in butter on either side. Serve with mushroom sauce (see p 114).

Stuffed potato roll

	USA	Imperial	Metric
potatoes	*2lb*	*2lb*	*1kg*
egg	*1*	*1*	*1*
butter	*4 tb*	*3 tb*	*3 tb*
mixed vegetable filling (see			
p 131)			
salt, pepper, to taste			

Boil the potatoes and mash while hot adding melted butter, egg, salt and pepper. The purée should be thick but not crumbly. If necessary add a little milk.

Spread the purée thickly on a damp cloth. Shape in an oblong. Down the centre lay the selected filling (see p 131) and, with the help of the cloth, surround with the potato pancake and join the edges firmly. Place the resulting roll seam downward on a buttered sheet. Brush with milk or beaten egg and bake for 30min in a hot oven.

Baked cabbage

	USA	Imperial	Metric
hard white cabbage	1 head	1 head	1 head
breadcrumbs	2 cup	4oz	120g
butter	½lb	4oz	120g
sour cream			
(half milk can be used)	3 cup	1½pt	¾l
salt, pepper, to taste			

Remove any loose leaves from the cabbage then cut out the heart leaving a firm outer layer of leaves to form a cup.

Chop the centre of the cabbage cutting off any thick leaf ends. Mix with breadcrumbs, salt and pepper and refill the cabbage shell. Put the cabbage into a casserole, sprinkle over with breadcrumbs, pour on the melted butter and half the cream. Cook in a hot oven for about 45min, until cabbage is quite soft. Before serving pour on the remaining cream and heat through.

It can be served with grated parmesan cheese, sprinkled over the gravy formed during the cooking.

Cabbage or carrot cutlets

	USA	Imperial	Metric
cabbage or carrot	2lb	2lb	1kg
semolina	1 cup	4oz	120g
milk	½ cup	4 fl oz	1dl
eggs, separated	3	3	3
breadcrumbs	4 tb	3 tb	3 tb
butter	4 tb	3 tb	3 tb
sugar	1 tsp	1 tsp	1 tsp
salt, to taste			

Finely chop cabbage or thinly slice carrot, put in a pan, cover with milk, add butter, salt and sugar. Braise, stirring occasionally, for 30–40min. Gradually add the semolina stirring all the time to break up lumps. Simmer for another 10min. Take the pan off heat, add beaten egg yolks, mix thoroughly and cool. Shape into flat, oblong cutlets, brush with white of egg and coat with breadcrumbs. Fry on both sides till browned and serve with sour cream or mushroom sauce (see p 84 or p 114).

Carrot braised with rice

	USA	Imperial	Metric
carrot	2lb	2lb	1kg
rice	2½ tb	2 tb	2 tb
butter	2½ tb	2 tb	2 tb
sugar	1 tsp	1 tsp	1 tsp
parsley	2 sprigs	2 sprigs	2 sprigs
salt, to taste			

Cut the washed and scraped carrots into rounds, put into a pan with rice, melted butter and sugar. Cover with water, lid firmly and braise for 40min in a medium oven. Ten minutes before serving add salt and finely chopped parsley.

Fried cucumber and sour cream

	USA	Imperial	Metric
cucumber	1 large	1 large	1 large
stock	½ cup	4 fl oz	1dl
sour cream	½ cup	4 fl oz	1dl
flour	½ tb	½ tb	½ tb
butter	1¼ tb	1 tb	1 tb
onion	1	1	1
salt, to taste			

Peel the cucumber, cut into pieces lengthwise, sprinkle with salt and leave for 30min. Chop the onion and fry in butter, add the pieces of cucumber and continue frying until the cucumber becomes soft. Add ½ tb flour, mix well with the onion, dilute with a little stock or water. Cook until it thickens and add cream. Heat through and serve with roast meat.

Stuffed beetroots (beets) or turnips

	USA	Imperial	Metric
beetroot (beet)	*4 medium*	*4 medium*	*4 medium*
soft crumb	*2 cup*	*4oz*	*120g*
milk	*5 tb*	*4 tb*	*4 tb*
egg	*1*	*1*	*1*
butter	*5 tb*	*2oz*	*25g*
breadcrumbs	*2½ tb*	*2 tb*	*2 tb*
salt, to taste			

Boil the beets in their skins and cool. Peel carefully and with a
sharp knife remove the centre leaving fairly thick walls. Chop

up the flesh of the beets, mix with bread soaked in milk, add beaten egg, butter, salt and mix thoroughly.

Fill the beetroot shells, brush over with butter, coat with breadcrumbs and brown in a hot oven for 20min.

Sweet corn with apples

	USA	Imperial	Metric
sweet corn, tinned or fresh	1 tin	1 tin	1 tin
onion	1	1	1
tomato purée	2½ tb	2 tb	2 tb
apples	2 large	2 large	2 large
sugar	1 tsp	1 tsp	1 tsp
butter	4 tb	2oz	60g
bread	4 slices	4 slices	4 slices
salt, to taste			

Chop and fry the onion. To the pan add sweet corn, tomato purée, salt, sugar; stir well and cook for 5min. Peel and core the apples, cut into quarters and simmer in a little water until soft but not overcooked. Fry the slices of bread in butter on both sides and onto each slice place some sweet corn decorated with 2 apple quarters.

Brussels sprouts in celery sauce

	USA	Imperial	Metric
sprouts	1lb	1lb	500g
For sauce:			
celery, chopped	1 stick	1 stick	1 stick
flour	1¼ tb	1 tb	1 tb
milk	½ cup	4 fl oz	1dl
butter	2½ tb	2 tb	2 tb
breadcrumbs	2½ tb	2 tb	2 tb
salt, to taste			

Cook the sprouts in salted water, boiling rapidly for 10min. Melt the butter, chop the celery and fry for 5min. Add flour

and brown, then gradually add hot milk and 2 or 3 tb of the
water in which the sprouts were cooked. Simmer the sauce for
a few minutes.

Drain the sprouts and mix with the sauce. Put in a fireproof
dish, cover with breadcrumbs and dot with butter. Brown in
a hot oven or under a grill.

Mushroom solyanka (baked)

	USA	Imperial	Metric
mushrooms	*1lb*	*1lb*	*500g*
cabbage	*2lb*	*2lb*	*1kg*
dill-pickle cucumbers	*3*	*3*	*3*
onion	*1*	*1*	*1*
tomato purée	*2½ tb*	*2 tb*	*2 tb*
sugar	*4 tsp*	*3 tsp*	*3 tsp*
butter	*2½ tb*	*2 tb*	*2 tb*
breadcrumbs	*4 tb*	*3 tb*	*3 tb*
vinegar	*1¼ tb*	*1 tb*	*1 tb*
bayleaf	*1*	*1*	*1*
salt, pepper, to taste			

Chop the cabbage and put in a pan with vinegar and barely
enough water to cover. Braise for an hour very gently. After
45min add the tomato purée, 2 sliced salted cucumbers, salt,
pepper, sugar and bayleaf. Simmer for another 15min.

Prepare the mushrooms; scald for 10min in boiling water
and drain. Slice and fry in butter. Remove the mushrooms and
in the same pan soften the chopped onion. Mix with the mushrooms, add the remaining sliced cucumber.

Spread a layer of cabbage in a buttered fireproof dish, cover
with the mushroom and onion and then put the remaining
cabbage on top. Sprinkle the surface with breadcrumbs and
brown in a hot oven.

STUFFED VEGETABLES

These are extremely popular in Russian cooking and the house-wife can choose from a number of fillings to use with baked potatoes, tomatoes, turnips, cabbage leaves, beetroot (beet) or marrow, which can then be served with a suitable sauce. These fillings are as follows:

Meat filling

Prepare the minced (ground) meat as for 'Golubtsy' (see p 93) and then use with any vegetable.

Meat and rice filling

Use half the quantity of the meat filling in the previous recipe, and replace the rest with boiled rice.

Rice and mushroom filling

	USA	Imperial	Metric
rice	*1 cup*	*6oz*	*180g*
onion	*2*	*2*	*2*
mushrooms	*½lb*	*8oz*	*240g*
butter	*4 tb*	*3 tb*	*3 tb*
salt, pepper, to taste			

Boil the rice and drain. Scald the mushrooms for 5min, slice and fry in butter. Mix with the rice. Add fried chopped onion, salt and pepper.

Mixed vegetable filling

	USA	Imperial	Metric
carrots	*3*	*3*	*3*
onions	*3*	*3*	*3*
celery	*2 sticks*	*2 sticks*	*2 sticks*
tomatoes	*2*	*2*	*2*

	USA	Imperial	Metric
butter	4 tb	3 tb	3 tb
parsley, chopped	2 tsp	2 tsp	2 tsp
salt, pepper, to taste			

NOTE: To this basic mixture can be added any vegetables in season such as peas, string beans, sweet peppers etc.

Finely chop the prepared vegetables and fry in butter. Add the peeled sliced tomatoes, salt, pepper and chopped parsley. Mix well and allow to cool before using, so that the butter can harden.

Vegetable golubtsy (cabbage leaves stuffed with vegetables)

	USA	Imperial	Metric
cabbage	1 small	1 small	1 small
carrots	3	3	3
onion	3	3	3
celery	1 stick	1 stick	1 stick
tomatoes	2 medium	2 medium	2 medium
parsley	1 sprig	1 sprig	1 sprig
sour cream	½ cup	4 fl oz	1 dl
tomato purée	2½ tb	2 tb	2 tb
butter	4 tb	3 tb	3 tb
salt, pepper, to taste			

Boil the cabbage just covered in salted water for 20min and drain. Separate the leaves, removing thick stalk ends. Reckoning 3 or 4 per person, lay cabbage leaves flat on a working surface. Onto each lay mixed vegetable filling (see p 131), roll up tightly (tie with thread if necessary) and brown quickly in butter.

Place in layers in a small casserole, add sour cream mixed with tomato purée, covered with a lid and cook in a fairly hot oven for 30min, basting several times during the cooking.

Stuffed baked turnip with cheese

	USA	Imperial	Metric
turnips	*8 medium*	*8 medium*	*8 medium*
semolina	*½ cup*	*4oz*	*120g*
milk	*½ cup*	*4 fl oz*	*1 dl*
sugar	*½ tb*	*½ tb*	*½ tb*
cheese, grated	*4 tb*	*3 tb*	*3 tb*
butter	*4 tb*	*3 tb*	*3 tb*
salt, pepper, to taste			

Thinly peel the turnips and boil in salted water until nearly
ready. Drain and carefully remove the flesh with a sharp knife
leaving a thin shell. Chop the turnip flesh and simmer until
quite soft, then mash. Meanwhile cook the semolina in milk

with a little sugar. Mix with the mashed turnip, 2 tb of butter, salt, pepper and half the cheese. Fill the turnip shells. Place these in a buttered dish, each turnip coated with butter and grated cheese. Cook in a hot oven for 25min.

7

Sweet

Some form of fruit is the Russian's favourite end to a meal.

Compote

Compote or stewed fruit, is served in different combinations as for instance prunes and orange; melon compote when the fruit is scalded, not cooked; mixed berry compote with raspberries, strawberries, currants, black and red, mixed in a salad bowl, hot syrup poured over and then the whole well chilled before serving. Compote is also made of grapes, which are peeled and covered in cold syrup with a dash of maraschino; or of any dried or frozen fruit.

Fresh berries and sweet wine

	USA	Imperial	Metric
mixed berries	*1½lb*	*1½lb*	*750g*
sugar	*1 cup*	*7oz*	*200g*
Madeira, marsala or sherry	*½ cup*	*4 fl oz*	*1dl*
cream	*½ cup*	*4 fl oz*	*1dl*

Mix the hulled or stoned berries in a bowl with the sugar, pour on the wine, stir without damaging the fruit and leave to macerate for 3hr. Serve well chilled with cream.

Strawberries Romanoff

	USA	Imperial	Metric
strawberries	1lb	1lb	500g
sugar	1 cup	7oz	200g
Curaçao	1¼ tb	1 tb	1 tb
orange juice	1¼ tb	1 tb	1 tb
cream	½ cup	4 fl oz	1 dl

Mix the strawberries with the sugar in a bowl. Pour on the Curaçao mixed with orange juice. Macerate for 2hr. Chill in a refrigerator and serve with whipped cream.

Kissel (sweetened fruit juice thickened with cornflour [cornstarch])

Jellies and mousses of any fruit flavour as well as chocolate, almond, vanilla blancmanges are constantly served. But kissel is the classical Russian sweet.

It can be made nearly solid, when it is apt to be rather cloying; semi-solid, the favourite way of serving it; or fairly liquid to be used as a hot fruit sauce.

Kissel is best made from the juice of tart raw berry such as blackcurrant or cranberry, diluted with twice its own volume of water and sweetened with its own volume of sugar. Tinned or bottled fruit can be used, in which case the amount of sugar must be greatly reduced. Prepared fruit juice is an easy way of making kissel, while in Russia one can even buy kissel cubes ready to dissolve in hot water.

Blackcurrant or cranberry kissel

	USA	Imperial	Metric
fruit	*2–3lb*	*2–3lb*	*1–1½kg*
sufficient to produce	*1 cup juice*	*½pt juice*	*¼l juice*
water	*2 cup*	*1pt*	*½l*
sugar	*1 cup*	*7oz*	*200g*
cornflour (cornstarch)	*2½ tb*	*2 tb*	*2 tb*

Rub the berries through a sieve to produce thick purée, add water to the purée, bring to the boil and strain. Put in the sugar and heat, stirring to ensure that it has completely dissolved; add cornflour (cornstarch) dissolved in a little cold water. Boil for 1–2min till the kissel begins to thicken. Pour into a bowl and chill. Serve with almond milk (see p 149).

Tinned fruit kissel

Proceed exactly as for fresh fruit kissel, except that sugar must be added to taste as this depends on the sweetness of the syrup. I always add the juice of ½ a lemon to give that slight tartness a true kissel should have.

Dried apricot kissel

	USA	Imperial	Metric
dried apricot	*1 cup*	*7oz*	*200g*
sugar	*1 cup*	*7oz*	*200g*
boiling water	*4 cup*	*2pt*	*1l*
cornflour (cornstarch)	*2½ tb*	*2 tb*	*2 tb*

Soak the apricots in boiling water for 2–3hr. Simmer in the same water on low heat for 30min till soft. Strain the liquid into a pan, rub the fruit through a sieve or liquidise and put the purée back into the juice together with the sugar. Boil till the sugar is completely melted, strain. Dissolve cornflour (cornstarch) in a little water, mix with the juice and boil for 2min. Chill.

Kissel of cherry syrup (or any other syrup)

	USA	Imperial	Metric
cherry syrup	1 cup	½pt	¼l
boiling water	2 cup	1pt	½l
sugar	2½ tb	2 tb	2 tb
cornflower (cornstarch)	2½ tb	2 tb	2 tb
citric acid, a pinch			

Mix the syrup and boiling water, add sugar and citric acid, bring to the boil. Stir in cornflour (cornstarch) dissolved in several tablespoons of cold water, boil for 2min until it begins to thicken. Chill.

Ice cream

Ice cream is extremely popular among Russians and is served in all shapes and flavours. In the centre of Moscow stands an 'Ice Cream Palace', its elaborate halls open till late at night. There seems always to be a queue of people waiting for vacant seats at the little tables, with menus offering a vast selection. A favourite flavour is blackcurrant, but there is also a full range of sundaes, cassata etc.

Apples, the fruit which kept best in the days before refrigeration, are the stand-by of classic Russian cooking and are used both as a sweet and as ingredients in other dishes.

Baked apples stuffed with nuts and rice

	USA	Imperial	Metric
apples, large	8	8	8
raisins	½ cup	3oz	90g
rice	½ cup	4oz	120g
walnuts, chopped	1 cup	2oz	60g
sugar	1 cup	8oz	240g
egg	1	1	1
butter	2½ tb	2 tb	2 tb

	USA	Imperial	Metric
cream	2½ tb	2 tb	2 tb
milk	½ cup	4 fl oz	1dl

Core the apples, removing a little of the flesh to make a larger opening. Cook the rice in milk until soft, with half the sugar. Mix in raisins, nuts, beaten egg and melted butter. Fill the hollowed apples and stand in a baking tin with a little water. Bake in a fairly hot oven for 40min or until apples are soft. Serve sprinkled with sugar and topped with cream.

Bread and apple babka

	USA	Imperial	Metric
apples	1lb	1lb	500g
milk	1 cup	8 fl oz	2dl
egg	1	1	1
white bread	10 slices	10 slices	300g
sugar	¾ cup	5oz	150g
butter	4 tb	3 tb	3 tb
mixed peel	2 tsp	2 tsp	2 tsp

Toast a couple of slices of bread or else dry them in a slow oven. Peel and core the apples, slice, add sugar and a little butter, simmer till cooked. Beat egg and milk together and soak the remaining slices of bread. With these line a soufflé dish.

Mix the cooked apples with the toast well crumbled in melted butter. Add mixed peel. Fill the lined dish and top with soaked bread. Bake in a medium oven for 30–40min. Leave for 10min in the soufflé dish to set, then turn out and if desired decorate with cherries or nuts.

A fruit sauce or cream can be served separately.

Airy apple

	USA	Imperial	Metric
apple	1lb	1lb	500g
sugar	½ cup	4oz	120g

	USA	Imperial	Metric
egg whites, chilled	4	4	4
sugar	$1\frac{1}{4}$ tb	*1 tb*	*1 tb*

Peel and core the apples; slice and bake in the oven in a very little water until soft. Rub through a fine sieve. Add sugar to the purée and simmer gently until the purée is thick enough not to run off the spoon. Meanwhile chill the egg whites in the refrigerator and whip until very firm. Fold the apple purée into the whipped whites, cutting through until thoroughly blended. Transfer to a buttered soufflé dish and bake in a fairly hot oven until the mixture has risen and browned.

Airy prunes

The same airy pudding is excellent made with prunes in which case the purée consists of:

	USA	Imperial	Metric
prunes	*1 cup*	*7oz*	*200g*
sugar	$\frac{1}{2}$ *cup*	*4oz*	*120g*

Simmer the prunes in cold water until absolutely soft. Drain, remove stones and sieve. Add sugar and proceed exactly as for apple (see previous recipe).

Orange fritters

	USA	Imperial	Metric
oranges	*2 large*	*2 large*	*2 large*
caster (granulated) sugar	*5 tb*	*4 tb*	*4 tb*
Curaçao	*1 tsp*	*1 tsp*	*1 tsp*
For batter			
flour	*1 cup*	*4 oz*	*120g*
egg	*1*	*1*	*1*
olive oil	$1\frac{1}{4}$ tb	*1 tb*	*1 tb*
salt	$\frac{1}{4}$ *tsp*	$\frac{1}{4}$ *tsp*	$\frac{1}{4}$ *tsp*
butter	*1 tsp*	*1 tsp*	*1 tsp*

Mix flour to absolute smoothness with olive oil, melted butter and salt. Beat in the egg yolk and gradually add a little warm water to produce a consistency of thick cream. Rest for an hour. Just before use add stiffly whipped white of egg.

Peel the oranges and divide into segments removing white pith and pips. Dip each segment into half the sugar then immediately into the batter. Deep fry in hot but not smoking oil.

Thoroughly drain the fritters or dry on absorbent paper, sprinkle with the remaining sugar mixed with Curaçao.

Baked cherry (blackcurrant or bilberry)

	USA	Imperial	Metric
morello cherries	2lb	2lb	1kg
sugar	1 cup	7oz	200g
egg	2	2	2
cream or sour cream	1½ cup	12 fl oz	3–4dl
cinnamon	1 tsp	1 tsp	1 tsp
flour	½ tb	½ tb	½ tb

Prepare the cherries by removing stones and stalks. Mix in half the sugar and leave to macerate for 30min.

Whip together cream, eggs, remaining sugar, flour and cinnamon until well blended and light. Fold into the cherries, place in a buttered dish and bake in a fairly hot oven for 20min.

Fresh plum bake

	USA	Imperial	Metric
plums	20	20	20
breadcrumbs	5 tb	4 tb	4 tb
eggs, separated	3	3	3
unsalted butter	2 tb	2 tb	2 tb
cinnamon	1 tsp	1 tsp	1 tsp
almond, ground	2½ tsp	2 tsp	2 tsp
sugar	⅔ cup	4–5oz	130g

Scald the plums in boiling water until skins burst; drain, peel, remove stones. Place in a pan with half the sugar, sprinkle with cinnamon, cover with a lid and boil quickly for not more than 5min, taking care not to burn. Beat together egg yolks and sugar until white and fluffy. Beat in the unsalted butter and ground almonds. Mix breadcrumbs with the cooled plums, add to the egg mixture and fold in the stiffly whipped whites.

Place in a buttered soufflé dish and bake in a fairly hot oven for 20min.

Apple charlotte made with rye bread

	USA	Imperial	Metric
rye bread (stale)	*1lb*	*1lb*	*500g*
butter	*½ cup*	*4oz*	*120g*
cloves	*2*	*2*	*2*

	USA	Imperial	Metric
cinnamon	½ tsp	½ tsp	½ tsp
lemon	½	½	½
mixed peel	1¼ tb	1 tb	1 tb
apple	1½lb	1½lb	750g
sugar	¾ cup	5oz	150g
sherry (optional)	1 sherry glass	1 sherry glass	1 sherry glass

Finely crumb the stale bread and lightly fry in melted butter. Add cinnamon, ground cloves, grated lemon peel, mixed peel and 1 tb sugar. Also sherry if used.

Butter the sides of the charlotte dish and sprinkle with sugar. Put first a layer of spiced crumbs, then a layer of very thinly sliced apples (peeled and cored). Sprinkle with sugar and repeat until the dish is filled, ending with a layer of crumbs. Press down well, dot with butter and cook in a moderate oven for about an hour, taking care not to burn. Serve with cream.

Walnut pudding

	USA	Imperial	Metric
eggs, separated	4	4	4
sugar	1 cup	7oz	200g
walnut, ground	1 cup	8oz	240g
butter	2½ tb	2 tb	2 tb
breadcrumbs	2½ tb	2 tb	2 tb

Whip together yolks, sugar and butter till white, gradually adding the ground walnuts. Chill the whites and then beat stiffly. Fold carefully into the walnut mixture. Transfer to a soufflé dish, well buttered and coated with breadcrumbs. Bake in a fairly hot oven for 45min. Serve with melted butter.

Blinchiki

These are small pancakes usually served with honey or else rolled over a filling of sweetened cottage cheese, apple (or any other fruit) purée or any kind of jam. They can also be filled with meat or rice and served with soup.

Batter

	USA	Imperial	Metric
flour	*2 cup*	*8oz*	*240g*
milk	*2½ cup*	*1pt*	*½l*
eggs, separated	*3*	*3*	*3*
butter	*2½ tb*	*2 tb*	*2 tb*
olive oil	*1 tsp*	*1 tsp*	*1 tsp*

Make a smooth batter of flour, milk, egg yolks and olive oil. Just before using add the well beaten whites. Fry in a buttered pan on one side, turn, spread filling, fold over and fry on both sides. Keep hot till served. Blinchiki must be small and very thin.

Oladyi

Small thick pancakes to be eaten with honey or golden syrup.

	USA	Imperial	Metric
flour	*2 cup*	*8oz*	*240g*
butter or oil	*1¼ tb*	*1 tb*	*1 tb*
egg	*1*	*1*	*1*
sugar	*1 tsp*	*1 tsp*	*1 tsp*
yeast	*½oz*	*½oz*	*15g*
milk	*1 cup*	*½pt*	*¼l*
salt	*½ tsp*	*½ tsp*	*½ tsp*

Dissolve the yeast in warm milk and gradually mix in the sifted flour. Cover with a cloth and set in a warm place for 30min, to rise. To the risen dough add beaten egg, salt, sugar and 1 tb of butter or olive oil. Once again cover with a cloth and leave to rise for another 30 or 40min.

Without disturbing the dough, moisten a tablespoon in cold water and put 1 tb at a time into a small pan coated with hot oil or butter. Fry on both sides.

Apple oladyi

This is prepared exactly as above, except that a couple of eating apples are peeled, cored, very thinly sliced and mixed into the risen dough just before frying the oladyi.

Almond oladyi

Another version is to use almond milk instead of plain milk in the preparation (see p 149).

Vareniki

These are small balls of pastry filled with cherries, bilberries or sweetened cottage cheese.

Pastry

	USA	Imperial	Metric
flour	2 cup	8oz	240g
egg	1	1	1
salt	1 pinch	1 pinch	1 pinch
cold water	1–2 tb	1–2 tb	1–2 tb

Into the sifted flour, mix egg and salt, gradually adding water to form a stiff dough. Knead to ensure that it is absolutely smooth. Roll out as thinly as possible on a floured board and cut into small rounds.

Cherry vareniki

	USA	Imperial	Metric
morello cherries	2 cup	1lb	500g
sugar	½ cup	4oz	120g

Mix the stoned cherries with the sugar and leave them to macerate for 1–2hr.

Onto each round of pastry (made in previous recipe) place one or two cherries, leaving the juice and sugar in the basin.

Join the edges of the pastry very firmly over the fruit, drop the vareniki a few at a time into boiling water. When they float up to the surface remove with a perforated spoon. Make a syrup of the sugar and cherry juice, adding a little water, and serve hot with the vareniki.

Blackcurrant jam, bilberries or cottage cheese, well drained and worked into a stiff paste with an egg and sugar, can also be used as fillings for vareniki.

Sweets made of *cottage cheese* (or *curd cheese*) are a Russian speciality.

Syrniki

	USA	Imperial	Metric
cottage cheese	*3 cup*	*12oz*	*360g*
eggs	*2*	*2*	*2*
butter, melted	*2½ tb*	*2 tb*	*2 tb*
sugar	*2½ tb*	*2 tb*	*2 tb*
cream	*2½ tb*	*2 tb*	*2 tb*
flour	*2½ tb*	*2 tb*	*2 tb*

Drain the cottage cheese, squeezing through a cloth or leaving under a press to extract moisture. Sieve or beat well to remove any lumps and, still beating, add eggs, cream, sugar and flour. Make a compact roll of the mixture and cut into thick slices. Then *either*:

Fry on both sides in hot oil or butter and serve with sour cream and sugar

or:

Drop into boiling water and remove with a perforated spoon when they float to the surface. Serve with sugar and melted butter or sour cream.

Cottage cheese bake

	USA	Imperial	Metric
cottage cheese	3 cup	12oz	360g
butter, melted	2½ tb	2 tb	2 tb
egg	1	1	1
cream	2½ tb	2 tb	2 tb
semolina	1¼ tb	1 tb	1 tb
raisins	½ cup	3oz	75g
vanilla	¼ tsp	¼ tsp	¼ tsp
candied peel	1¼ tb	1 tb	1 tb
breadcrumbs	1¼ tb	1 tb	1 tb

Prepare the cottage cheese as in previous recipe, add melted butter, egg well beaten with sugar, semolina, raisins, candied peel and vanilla. Butter an oven dish, dust with breadcrumbs. Level the mixture into it and brush the surface with butter. Bake in a fairly hot oven for 30min until browned. Serve with hot fruit sauce.

Cottage cheese pudding

	USA	Imperial	Metric
eggs, separated	4	4	4
cottage cheese	3 cup	12oz	360g
caster (granulated) sugar	1½ cup	10oz	300g
butter	1 cup	8oz	240g
cream, sour or fesh	1 cup	8oz	2dl
vanilla	½ tsp	½ tsp	½ tsp
breadcrumbs	2½ tb	2 tb	2 tb

Drain the cottage cheese of all liquid and sieve. Beat yolks, sugar and vanilla till white and fluffy, add butter, cream and cottage cheese. Blend thoroughly. Whip the egg whites into stiff peaks, fold carefully into the sour cream mixture. Turn the pudding into a basin, cover firmly and steam for 1½–2hr.

SAUCES TO SERVE WITH PUDDINGS AND SWEETS

Sweet wine sauce

	USA	Imperial	Metric
marsala or Madeira	*2 cup*	*¾pt*	*4dl*
caster (granulated) sugar	*1 cup*	*7oz*	*200g*
cinnamon	*1 pinch*	*1 pinch*	*1 pinch*
cloves	*3*	*3*	*3*

Mix all ingredients and bring gently to the boil. When the sugar is completely melted, strain and serve.

Fresh fruit or berry sauce (1pt sauce)

	USA	Imperial	Metric
fruit (cherries, plums,			
raspberries, strawberries)	*½lb*	*8oz*	*225g*
Madeira	*6 tb*	*6 tb*	*6 tb*
sugar	*½ cup*	*3–4oz*	*100g*
cinnamon	*1 pinch*	*1 pinch*	*1 pinch*
cornflour (cornstarch)	*2 tsp*	*2 tsp*	*2 tsp*
water	*2 cup*	*1pt*	*4dl*

Cherries and plums should be boiled in half the amount of water, stoned, sieved, and returned to the pan. Raspberries and strawberries should have juice squeezed out through a cloth or be rubbed through a very fine sieve and then the water added to the purée.

Add Madeira, cinnamon and sugar to the liquid. Bring to the boil. Dissolve the cornflour (cornstarch) in the remaining water, add to the sauce and boil until it thickens slightly.

Dried apricot sauce

	USA	Imperial	Metric
dried apricot	*1 cup*	*6oz*	*180g*
sugar	*4 tb*	*2 oz*	*60g*

	USA	Imperial	Metric
sweet white wine	¼ cup	6 tb	6 tb
water	2 cup	1pt	4dl

Boil the apricots in half the amount of water until soft. Rub through a fine sieve and return to the syrup. Add sugar, the rest of the water and boil for 5min. Remove from heat and stir in the wine, previously brought to the boil.

Almond milk

This is especially good with kissel. A quick way of preparing it is to use 2 tsp of almond flavouring and 1 tsp caster sugar to a cup of milk. Boil up and chill.

The classic way to make it is as follows:

	USA	Imperial	Metric
sweet almonds	*1 cup*	*4oz*	*120g*
bitter almonds	*5*	*5*	*5*
caster (granulated) sugar	*½ cup*	*3oz*	*120g*
milk	*2 cup*	*1pt*	*½l*

Scald the almonds, remove skins and grind. Add the milk, 1 tb at a time. Boil up and simmer for 5–10min. Strain, add sugar and stir until it has completely melted. Serve cold.

8

The Supper Table

The table set for a substantial supper might well consist of a selection of zakousky, fish in aspic, a plate of pirozhki or a meat pirog. If a hot dish is required then pelmeni, or an egg dish or buckwheat and butter is offered. Probably kissel is served as a sweet, some biscuits or krendel with the tea, with sweets to pass round. Everyday suppers would naturally be far less elaborate with only one or two dishes.

Aspic

Stock used for aspic should be heated before the dissolved gelatine is added. Then it is brought to the boil and strained through a cloth into a basin in which it can cool before being used to coat the fish or meat or vegetable.

Aspic can be clarified by the addition of a beaten white of egg (mixed in a little cold stock with 1 tb of lemon juice), then add to the hot stock together with the gelatine. Bring to near boiling on low heat and leave to stand in the pan for 20 min before straining, being careful not to disturb the residue.

I find that 1 tsp of brandy added to the aspic greatly enriches the flavour.

Fish in aspic

	USA	Imperial	Metric
fish steaks	*4*	*4*	*4*
trimmings for stock	*½lb*	*8oz*	*240g*
water	*2pt*	*2pt*	*1l*
onion	*1*	*1*	*1*
celery	*1 stick*	*1 stick*	*1 stick*
carrot	*2*	*2*	*2*
bayleaf	*1*	*1*	*1*
peppercorns	*4*	*4*	*4*
salt	*½ tsp*	*½ tsp*	*½ tsp*
cloves	*3*	*3*	*3*
parsley	*2 sprigs*	*2 sprigs*	*2 sprigs*
lemon	*1*	*1*	*1*
egg, hard-boiled	*1*	*1*	*1*
gelatine	*½oz*	*½oz*	*15g*

NOTE: Cod, halibut, salmon, turbot or hake may be used.

Chop the onion and celery but leave carrots whole; simmer with fish trimmings, bayleaf, peppercorns, salt and cloves for 40min in the water to make stock. Add the pieces of fish and cook for 15–20min without breaking. Remove these with a perforated spoon and set aside to cool. Remove the carrots from the stock and leave to one side. Strain the remaining stock which should have reduced by about half.

Soften the gelatine and dissolve in a little cold water, add to the boiling stock, stirring constantly. Strain through a cheese-cloth, allowing it to drip through without stirring.

Slice the carrots lengthways, arrange decoratively at the bottom of a mould. When the aspic is strained, just cover the carrots and set in a refrigerator to cool for 30 min until the aspic is set.

Arrange the fish on the aspic, decorate with lemon slices and parsley, cover with aspic and return to the refrigerator. If the mould is not wide enough to take all the fish in one layer, repeat the process and finally leave in the refrigerator for 2–3hr until the aspic is quite hard and chilled.

Pass a knife round the edge of the mould, place the serving dish over it and turn upside down for the aspic to slide out.

Tongue (or ham) in aspic

	USA	Imperial	Metric
tongue	2lb	2lb	1kg
onion	1	1	1
carrot	1	1	1
bouquet garni	1	1	1
peppercorns	4	4	4
salt	½ tsp	½ tsp	½ tsp
gelatine	1 pkt	1oz	30g
cucumber	1 small	1 small	1 small
tomato	4 small	4 small	4 small
egg, hard-boiled	1	1	1
stock	2 cup	1pt	4dl

Boil the tongue with the vegetables and bouquet garni for 1hr or until soft. Remove and drain the meat. Strain the stock, cool and remove the fat from the surface. Take the stock and prepare aspic (see p 151).

Skin and slice the tongue. If ham is used reckon on 1 fairly thick slice per person. Lay the fairly thick slices on a dish. Decorate each slice with some hard-boiled egg, cucumber, tomato. Cover with aspic in several applications, putting the dish into the refrigerator for the aspic to set between each application. Finally leave to chill and harden for 2hr in the refrigerator. Then carefully cut out each separate slice with its own aspic. Serve with a salad of red cabbage.

PIROG, PIROZHKI AND KOULEBIAKA

These pies and patties are probably the quintessence of Russian cooking. The root of the word is the Russian 'pir', meaning 'feast'. Pirozhki are small patties served with soup, as appetisers, or offered with tea or coffee at any time. A pirog is a larger, circular or rectangular, fairly flat pie, with pastry top and bottom. Both are baked with a variety of fillings (see pp 156–9). The pastry used is either straightforward short crust, puff or flaky, or else dough made with yeast or with sour cream. A pirog, especially those made with fruit or jam (see p 184) can also be open, like a large tart, latticed with pastry.

Yeast dough

	USA	Imperial	Metric
plain flour	*1lb*	*1lb*	*500g*
milk	*1 cup*	*½pt*	*2dl*
fresh yeast	*½oz*	*½oz*	*15g*
butter	*6 tb*	*3oz*	*90g*
eggs	*2*	*2*	*2*
sugar	*1¼ tb*	*1 tb*	*1 tb*
salt, a pinch			

Put half the flour into a basin with 1 tb of sugar. Dissolve the yeast in warm milk and gradually add to the flour, stirring constantly to avoid the formation of any lumps. Cover with a cloth and stand in a warm place to rise until it doubles its volume (30–40min).

Beat in 2 eggs, pinch of salt and melted butter. Stir until all is incorporated and then knead, while adding the remaining flour. The dough should not be too stiff. Continue kneading until the dough no longer sticks to hands or to the sides of the basin. Cover, put in a warm place to rise once again.

Roll out the dough and make the pirog or pirozhki leaving them on the baking sheet for a further 30–40min until risen again.

Pirog with yeast dough

Roll out half the pastry into a circular or rectangular shape. Place on a buttered baking sheet and spread the filling, leaving a narrow border of pastry. Roll out the second half of the pastry and place over the filling. Turn up the edges of the pastry to make a firm rim, which can then be pinched into decorative pleats. Prick the top with a fork. Leave to rise. With any pastry scraps make a design and decorate the top. Brush with beaten egg or milk and bake in a fairly hot oven for 30min, until browned.

Pirozhki with yeast dough, puff or shortcrust pastry

When the pastry is rolled cut out small rounds. On one half place 1 tsp of filling, cover with another round, dampening the edges with cold water and pinching together firmly. If different fillings are used, make one sort round, another sort boat-shaped. If yeast dough is used leave pirozhki to rise. Bake in hot oven for 20min.

Deep fried pirozhki

Pirozhki made with yeast dough (see previous page) are often deep fried. In that case double the amount of milk in the dough and halve the yeast, otherwise the pirozhki come out too dry. The fat should be very hot and the pirozhki left to cook for about 5min each side.

Sour cream pastry

	USA	Imperial	Metric
flour	1lb	1lb	500g
sour cream	1 cup	8oz	240g
butter	2½ tb	2 tb	2 tb
eggs	2	2	2

Fillings used in pirog, pirozhki or blinchiki

	USA	Imperial	Metric
sugar	*1¼ tb*	*1 tb*	*1 tb*
salt	*½ tsp*	*½ tsp*	*½ tsp*

NOTE: This pastry can be prepared without sour cream in which case double the amount of butter used.

Place the flour in a heap in the basin. Make a hollow in the centre and pour in sour cream, salt and sugar. Add softened or clarified butter. Beat the eggs and mix all together to form a firm dough.

Make a ball of the dough, cover with a cloth and leave in the refrigerator for at least 40min. Roll out thinly. This makes about 25 pirozhki or 1 pirog.

The quantities are for one pirog, using pastry made with 1lb flour. Half the amount of filling required if pirozhki are to be made. These fillings can also be used with blinchiki (see p 143).

Minced (ground) meat

	USA	Imperial	Metric
minced (ground) beef	*1lb*	*1lb*	*500g*
butter	*4 tb*	*3 tb*	*3 tb*
eggs, hard-boiled	*2*	*2*	*2*
onion	*1 small*	*1 small*	*1 small*
parsley	*2 sprigs*	*2 sprigs*	*2 sprigs*
salt, pepper, to taste			

Mince (grind) the raw meat finely and brown in 1 tb butter. Separately soften the chopped onion in some butter and mix with the meat. Add chopped hard-boiled egg, salt, pepper and chopped parsley. Mix in 1 tb melted butter and moisten with a little stock if the filling appears to be too dry.

Cabbage filling

	USA	Imperial	Metric
white cabbage	1lb	1lb	500g
eggs, hard-boiled	2	2	2
sugar	1 tsp	1 tsp	1 tsp
butter	5 tb	2oz	60g
salt, pepper, to taste			

Finely chop and scald the cabbage. Rinse in cold water and squeeze dry. Put in a saucepan with melted butter and simmer for 15min till soft, stirring at intervals. Add salt, pepper, sugar, and chopped hard-boiled eggs. Mix well. The filling is much easier to use when cold and the butter has hardened.

Sauerkraut filling

	USA	Imperial	Metric
sauerkraut	1lb	1lb	500g
butter	2½ tb	2 tb	2 tb
onion	2	2	2
dried mushroom	¼ cup	1oz	30g
salt, pepper, to taste			

Rinse the sauerkraut, scald and drain. Chop it finely and simmer with 1 tb melted butter until soft. Chop and soften the onion in 1 tb butter. Soak the dried mushroom for 1hr before using, then bring to the boil, drain well, chop and mix with the onion. Add salt and pepper and fry all together for 3–4min. Mix with the sauerkraut.

Egg and rice filling

	USA	Imperial	Metric
rice	½ cup	4oz	120g
eggs, hard-boiled	3	3	3
butter	4 tb	3 tb	3 tb
salt	1 tsp	1 tsp	1 tsp
parsley or dill	3 sprigs	3 sprigs	3 sprigs

Cook the rice on low heat in salted water, two fingers above the surface of the rice, for 12–15min. Drain well and mix in a bowl with chopped hard-boiled eggs, melted butter, salt and chopped parsley or dill.

Mushroom filling

	USA	Imperial	Metric
fresh mushrooms	*1lb*	*1lb*	*500g*
butter	*5 tb*	*2oz*	*60g*
onion	*1*	*1*	*1*
garlic (optional)	*½ clove*	*½ clove*	*½ clove*
double (heavy) cream or			
sour cream	*5 tb*	*4 tb*	*4 tb*
salt, pepper, to taste			

Scald the mushrooms, drain well, slice and fry in 3 tb butter. Chop the onion and soften in remaining butter with the crushed clove or garlic. Mix with the mushrooms, add salt, pepper and cream. Cover with a lid and simmer for 10min. Cool.

Mushroom and buckwheat filling

	USA	Imperial	Metric
buckwheat or rice	*½ cup*	*7oz*	*200g*
fresh mushrooms	*¼lb*	*4oz*	*120g*
onion	*1*	*1*	*1*
butter	*5 tb*	*4 tb*	*4 tb*
salt, pepper, to taste			

Slice and boil the mushrooms for a few minutes in salted water. Remove with a perforated spoon to drain and use the mushroom flavoured water to cook the rice or buckwheat. Fry the chopped onion in 1 tb butter. Add the mushrooms and fry for 3 or 4min. Mix with the cooked rice or buckwheat and remaining butter, melted. Adjust salt and pepper to taste.

Fish filling

	USA	Imperial	Metric
fish fillet	$\frac{1}{2}$ *lb*	$\frac{1}{2}$ *lb*	*240g*
butter	*2$\frac{1}{2}$ tb*	*2 tb*	*2 tb*
onion	*1 medium*	*1 medium*	*1 medium*
eggs, hard-boiled	*2*	*2*	*2*
salt	$\frac{1}{2}$ *tsp*	$\frac{1}{2}$ *tsp*	$\frac{1}{2}$ *tsp*

Skin the fish fillets and cut up finely, salt well and fry in half
the butter. Chop and fry the onion in remaining butter and
add to the fish. Chop the hard-boiled eggs and mix.

KOULEBIAKA

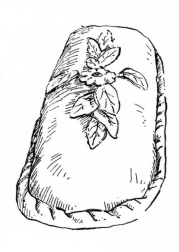

Rastegai (patties made of yeast dough)

	USA	Imperial	Metric
fresh herring	*2 large*	*2 large*	*2 large*
or salmon	$\frac{1}{2}$ *lb*	$\frac{1}{2}$ *lb*	*240g*
onion	*2 medium*	*2 medium*	*2 medium*
butter	*5 tb*	*4 tb*	*4 tb*
salt, pepper, to taste			

Prepare the dough (see p 154) roll and cut into 8 or 12 fairly
large rounds. Chop the onion and fry until soft in half the

butter. Fillet the herring, carefully removing skin and bones. Divide the fried onion, according to the number of pastry rounds placing some on each. On top of the onion lay pieces of the prepared fish, spreading each with softened butter. Brush the edges of the pastry with water or ale and pinch together firmly leaving a small gap at the top. Let them stand for ½hr and then bake in a fairly hot oven for 20–25min.

Koulebiaka

Koulebiaka differs from an ordinary broad flat pirog in its shape which is high and narrow and its pastry which is richer. It is usually filled with different fillings in separate layers, as for instance one of savoury rice, then a layer of meat or fish topped with a layer of hard-boiled egg or mushroom. To prevent the inside of the pastry becoming moist a 'dry' layer of rice, semolina or buckwheat is used to sandwich the more juicy main layers. When made with puff or flaky pastry then very thin dry pancakes, of a flour and water batter are cooked and used as a lining. Pastry for koulebiaka is rolled slightly thicker than for a pirog in view of the larger amount of filling.

A quick flaky pastry can be made as follows:

	USA	Imperial	Metric
flour	*1lb*	*1lb*	*500g*
butter	*1½ cup*	*12oz*	*360g*
egg	*1*	*1*	*1*
lemon juice	*1 tsp*	*1 tsp*	*1 tsp*
salt	*½ tsp*	*½ tsp*	*½ tsp*
water	*7½ tb*	*6 tb*	*6 tb*

Sift the flour into a basin and add chilled butter cut into small pieces. Rub together with finger tips until crumbly. Make a hollow in the centre and put in salt, water, egg and lemon juice. Knead the mixture well. Roll the pastry into a ball, cover with a cloth and chill in a refrigerator for ½hr before using.

This amount is for the koulebiaka given in the next recipe.

Classic koulebiaka (serves 6–8)

	USA	Imperial	Metric
salmon	¾lb	12oz	360g
rice	¾ cup	4oz	120g
butter	5 tb	4 tb	4 tb
eggs, hard-boiled	3	3	3
onion	1 medium	1 medium	1 medium
mushroom	½lb	8oz	240g
dill-weed	2 tsp	2 tsp	2 tsp
salt	1 tsp	1 tsp	1 tsp
raw egg	1	1	1

First shake the rice with ½ tb melted butter in a frying pan over low heat until each grain is coated then cook in water, two fingers above the level of the rice, very slowly until all the water is absorbed and the rice is light and fluffy. Flake the salmon (either raw or cooked) and mix with the rice.

Scald the mushrooms, slice finely and fry with the dill weed and chopped onion. Mix in hard-boiled eggs finely chopped and salt. Roll out thinly half the flaky pastry (see p 160) in a rectangle. Place on a buttered baking sheet and along the centre lay the thin dry pancakes as a lining. Spread on a layer of salmon and rice, then the egg and mushroom, finally another layer of salmon and rice. Cover completely with thin pancakes. Roll out the second half of the pastry slightly longer and broader than the first. Brush the edges of the pastry with beaten raw egg. Cover the filling with the second half of the pastry and turn the bottom edge up over the top one to form a ledge. Seal firmly, pleating with finger tips.

Make 2 or 3 incisions along the top to let out the steam and decorate the top with a design made with the remaining scraps of pastry. Brush the top only with beaten egg and insert 1 tsp of melted butter into each incision.

Bake in the centre of a preheated fairly hot oven for 40–50 min. If the top browns too quickly, cover with foil until the bottom layer is cooked through.

Koulebiaka is served hot but is also good heated up on the following day. It can be made beforehand and re-heated for 15 or 20min before serving. To prevent the crust from hardening cover with a damp cloth.

It can also be made by rolling the pastry out in one large oblong and then folding it over the layers of filling, baking it sealed side downwards.

Siberian pelmeni

Small meat-filled dumplings, best cooked in concentrated beef stock and served hot with melted butter and sour cream.

	USA	Imperial	Metric
meat (half beef and half pork)	¾lb	12oz	360g
onion	1	1	1
flour	2 cup	8oz	240g
eggs, separated	2	2	2
concentrated stock	5 cup	2pt	1l
sugar	1 pinch	1 pinch	1 pinch
water	½ cup	4 fl oz	1dl
salt, pepper, to taste			

Mince (grind) the meat finely and mix with finely chopped raw onion, salt and pepper. Add 1 tb of cold water to bind.

Mix sifted flour, beaten egg yolks and the water with 1 tsp salt and a pinch of sugar to form a stiff dough. Roll out thinly on a floured board and cut into small rounds. Onto one side of each round place ½ tsp of filling.

Using the beaten white of egg, brush the edges of each round and fold over. Pinch together very firmly otherwise the filling will be lost in the bouillon. Chill in the refrigerator for 30min. Fifteen minutes before serving drop into the rapidly boiling stock. Cook for 5–10min (depending on the size of the pelmeni) until they float to the surface. Take out with a perforated spoon and keep warm until all are cooked. Rapidly reduce the bouillon to a cupful. Pour this over the pelmeni in a deep dish and separately serve melted butter and sour cream.

Pelmeni with ham and mushroom

Proceed as for Siberian pelmeni but prepare a ham filling:

	USA	Imperial	Metric
mushrooms	*¼lb*	*4oz*	*120g*
ham	*½lb*	*8oz*	*240g*
onion	*1 small*	*1 small*	*1 small*
butter	*1 tb*	*1 tb*	*1 tb*

Scald and slice the mushrooms. Chop and fry the onion in butter together with the mushrooms and mix with chopped ham.

Ukranian pelmeni

These are prepared as the other pelmeni but filled with stoned cherries, plums or bilberries mixed with sugar in the proportion of 4 to 1. Serve with cream and sugar.

EGGS

Supper or breakfast are the meals at which eggs are generally eaten. Besides all the usual methods of cooking, ie boiled, poached, fried etc, they are often used to provide tasty hot dishes such as:

Egg and fresh herring

	USA	Imperial	Metric
herring	*2 large*	*2 large*	*2 large*
sour cream	*½ cup*	*4oz*	*1dl*
eggs	*4*	*4*	*4*
butter, melted	*5 tb*	*4 tb*	*4 tb*
onion	*1 medium*	*1 medium*	*1 medium*
salt, pepper, to taste			

Fillet the herrings, removing all possible bones and skin. Sprinkle with salt and pepper, coat with flour and fry in butter on both sides. Chop the onion and fry separately. Beat the eggs with the cream and mix with the onion. Lay the fish fillets in a well buttered fireproof dish, cover with the egg and cream mixture and bake in a hot oven for 10min until the eggs are cooked through.

Salmon omelette

	USA	Imperial	Metric
eggs	*4–6*	*4–6*	*4–6*
salmon (or small tin)	*¼lb*	*4oz*	*120g*
milk	*2½ tb*	*2 tb*	*2 tb*
butter	*2½ tb*	*2 tb*	*2 tb*
salt, pepper, to taste			

Flake the salmon, removing any skin and bones. Beat the eggs and milk with salt and pepper. Mix in the salmon and cook in butter melted in omelette pan until the eggs thicken.

Apple omelette

	USA	Imperial	Metric
eggs	*4–6*	*4–6*	*4–6*
eating apples	*2lb*	*2lb*	*1kg*
butter	*2½ tb*	*2 tb*	*2 tb*
salt, to taste			

Peel, core and thinly slice the apples. Fry them gently in butter in the omelette pan. Over them pour the beaten eggs, salted to taste, and cook until the eggs thicken.

Egg cutlets

	USA	Imperial	Metric
eggs, hard-boiled	*5*	*5*	*5*
eggs, separated	*2*	*2*	*2*
whole egg	*1*	*1*	*1*

	USA	Imperial	Metric
parsley, chopped	1¼ tb	1 tb	1 tb
breadcrumbs	½ cup	2oz	60g
salt, to taste			

White sauce

	USA	Imperial	Metric
milk	1½ cup	12oz	3dl
flour	2½ tb	2 tb	2 tb
butter	2½ tb	2 tb	2 tb

Make a thick sauce of flour and butter, gradually adding hot milk and salt to taste, cook gently for 5–10min. Add 2 beaten raw yolks and the hard-boiled eggs not too finely chopped. Mix in chopped parsley. Place the mixture on a buttered plate to cool, brushing the surface with melted butter to prevent a skin forming.

When the mixture is cold take 1 tb at a time, smooth into egg-shaped cutlets, brush with beaten egg whites to which a whole egg has been added and coat the cutlets with breadcrumbs. Repeat this process to form a thick coating and fry in hot butter until crisp. Serve with green salad.

Stuffed eggs and potato purée

	USA	Imperial	Metric
eggs, hard-boiled	4	4	4
egg, raw	1	1	1
cheese, grated	5 tb	1oz	30g
ham (or mushroom), chopped	5 tb	2oz	60g
white bread	1 slice	1 slice	1 slice
onion	½ medium	½ medium	½ medium
parsley, chopped	1 tsp	1 tsp	1 tsp
milk in stuffing	1¼ tb	1 tb	1 tb

Potato purée

	USA	Imperial	Metric
potato	1lb	1lb	500g
milk	½ cup	4oz	1dl
butter	2½ tb	2 tb	2 tb
salt, to taste			

Shell the hard-boiled eggs and cut in half lengthwise. Remove the yolk and part of the white leaving an enlarged oblong hollow. Mix chopped yolks, whites, ham or fried mushroom, parsley, salt. Chop the onion finely, soften in butter, mix with crustless bread soaked in a little milk and one raw egg. Into this mix the egg and ham then carefully top the emptied whites smoothing so that each looks like a complete egg.

Make the potato purée and spread a layer in a fireproof dish. Arrange the stuffed eggs on the potato, cover the surface with grated cheese and sprinkle with melted butter. Brown in a hot oven for 10–15min.

Pashtet of leftovers

> *leftovers (meat, chicken or game)*
> *the same volume of bread soaked in milk*
> *1 hard-boiled egg*
> *2–3 tb melted butter*
> *shortcrust pastry (see p 184)*
> *salt, pepper and chopped parsley, to taste*

The quantity of soaked bread depends on the amount of leftovers to be used. The bread is then mixed with finely chopped onion and hard-boiled egg and seasoned to taste. Put the pieces of meat or chicken between two layers of bread forcemeat on a thinly rolled rectangle of shortcrust pastry, cover with another rectangle of pastry, pour the melted butter through incisions in the top of the pie and bake in a fairly hot oven for 30min.

VATROUSHKI

These are small open patties with a cottage cheese filling. They can also be filled with berries or jam.

Cottage cheese filling

	USA	Imperial	Metric
cottage cheese	*1lb*	*1lb*	*500g*
egg yolks	*2*	*2*	*2*
sugar	*1 cup*	*7oz*	*200g*
butter, melted	*1 tb*	*1 tb*	*1 tb*

Rub the well drained cottage cheese through a sieve, beat in the yolks and sugar. Mix well and add the melted butter.

For a large vatroushka I add a handful of raisins, 2 tb mixed peel, 2 tb vodka (lemon juice or a little vanilla essence can be used instead) and scatter a handful of peeled roughly chopped almonds over the surface.

Vatroushki with yeast dough, baked

Prepare the dough (see p 154). When the pastry has been rolled out, divide into balls the size of a large walnut, space out on a baking sheet and leave for 20min to rise.

Make a deep hollow in the centre of each and fill with whatever filling has been chosen, leaving the top open. Brush the pastry with beaten egg or milk and bake in a hot oven for 15min.

Vatroushki with yeast dough, fried

NOTE: These are usually done with minced (ground) meat filling (see p 156) and known as Belyashi.

Prepare the dough (see p 154). When the pastry has been rolled cut into fairly large rounds. Put a little filling in the centre and raise the edge of the pastry to make a border level with the filling. Fry in hot oil, the open side first, on medium heat for about 5min on each side.

Large vatroushka of Moscow pastry, baked

The quantities given are for a medium-sized flan ring, using the cottage cheese filling.

Moscow pastry

	USA	Imperial	Metric
self-raising flour	2 cup	8oz	240g
sugar	½ cup	4oz	120g
egg	1 large	1 large	1 large
butter	½ cup	4oz	120g

Mix flour, sugar and chopped chilled butter together with fingertips until blended and crumbly. Add the egg and mix thoroughly until a fairly dry, soft dough results. Roll out on a floured board fairly thickly and line a medium-sized flan ring set on a greased, floured sheet, with the edges of the pastry well above the edges of the flan ring. Spread the filling evenly over the pastry, sprinkle with chopped almonds and bake in a preheated moderate oven for 30min, until the pastry is well browned. Allow to cool before removing from the flan ring.

Syrniki with potato

	USA	Imperial	Metric
cottage cheese	1lb	1lb	500g
potatoes	1½lb	1½lb	750g
egg	1	1	1
butter	4 tb	3 tb	3 tb
sugar	2½ tb	2 tb	2 tb
sour cream	½ cup	4oz	1dl
flour	1 cup	4oz	120g
salt	½ tsp	½ tsp	½ tsp

Peel the potatoes and boil in salted water, drain and mash. Drain the cottage cheese of all moisture, sieve to remove lumps and mix with the mashed potato. Beat in the raw egg, salt, sugar and half the flour. Stir well to form a stiff paste. Place on a floured board and flatten into thick rounds. Coat with flour and fry in butter on each side until golden-brown. Serve hot with sour cream well chilled.

Syrniki can also be served sweet in which case double the amount of sugar and add a handful of raisins.

Cottage cheese and spinach bake

	USA	Imperial	Metric
cottage cheese	*1lb*	*1lb*	*500g*
sour cream	*1 cup*	*8oz*	*2dl*
eggs, separated	*3*	*3*	*3*
sugar	*2½ tb*	*2 tb*	*2 tb*
semolina	*2½ tb*	*2 tb*	*2 tb*
butter	*2½ tb*	*2 tb*	*2 tb*
breadcrumbs	*2½ tb*	*2 tb*	*2 tb*
spinach	*½lb*	*8oz*	*240g*
cheese, grated	*4 tb*	*3 tb*	*3 tb*

Thoroughly drain the cottage cheese, rub through a sieve to remove any lumps, mix in egg yolks, sugar, salt and semolina. Stir well. Wash and drain the spinach and chop finely. Mix with the cottage cheese. Whip whites of eggs till firm and fold into the mixture. Transfer to a buttered fireproof dish, sprinkle with breadcrumbs and grated cheese. Bake for 20min in fairly hot oven. Serve with melted butter and cold sour cream.

Cottage cheese with mixed peel

Prepare as for previous recipe only instead of spinach use 4 or 5 tb mixed peel, 2 tb raisins and extra 6 tb sugar. Serve with hot fruit syrup or jam.

Cottage cheese with almonds

Instead of mixed peel use chopped roasted almonds.

Cheese cutlets

	USA	Imperial	Metric
grated cheese	*2 cup*	*8oz*	*240g*
eggs, separated	*2*	*2*	*2*
breadcrumbs	*4 tb*	*3 tb*	*3 tb*
sour cream	*1 cup*	*8oz*	*2dl*
oil for frying			

Whip the egg whites until they stand in peaks, mix lightly with grated cheese. Take 1 tb at a time, roll into balls and set on a dish. Chill in the refrigerator for at least 30min. Then coat each hardened ball with breadcrumbs, dip into the beaten yolks and once again coat with breadcrumbs. Flatten and fry in hot oil for 2–3min until golden brown all over.

RUSSIAN USE OF CEREAL

'Kasha' is a word that cannot be translated. It implies a cooked cereal—rice, buckwheat, semolina, pearl barley. 'Kasha' can be a familiar sweet milk pudding, or else it can be boiled in salted water on low heat or baked in a cool oven until each grain is cooked and separate, and then used as a vegetable or eaten as a dish with melted butter. 'Kasha' applies to semolina baked with raisins or crushed wheat braised with pumpkin. Rice when used as a vegetable is called 'plov' on Russian menus and is adapted from Caucasian cuisine, but it becomes 'kasha' if used as a sweet. Northern Russians relied on the indigenous buckwheat, an acquired taste for non-Russians, although as 'kache' it is the obligatory accompaniment to suckling pig according to Escoffier.

Buckwheat kasha (Grechnevaya kasha)

This quantity is enough for four if used as a vegetable. If used as a dish on its own the quantity should be increased by half.

	USA	Imperial	Metric
buckwheat	½ *cup*	*4oz*	*120g*
salt	*1 tsp*	*1 tsp*	*1 tsp*
butter	*2½ tb*	*2 tb*	*2 tb*
water	*2pt*	*2pt*	*1l*

Melt the butter in a pan and cook the buckwheat in it on low heat until each grain is well coated with butter and slightly browned. In a small casserole bring the water to the boil with 1 tsp salt. Pour in the buckwheat ensuring that it only fills half the casserole, as it swells in cooking. Cover the pan with a lid and stand in a baking dish in an inch of water in a very low oven. Cook for 2hr or until the water in the casserole is completely absorbed. Turn out the oven and leave the casserole in it for another 20min. The buckwheat should be dry and fluffy.

Buckwheat kasha and egg

To the kasha in the previous recipe add 3 or 4 thinly sliced hard-boiled eggs and mix with another 2 tb melted butter.

Buckwheat mushroom and onion

To the cooked buckwheat add ¼lb mushrooms fried with 1 chopped onion. Add ½ cup cream and bake for 20 min in a moderate oven.

Buckwheat and cottage cheese

	USA	Imperial	Metric
buckwheat	*1 cup*	*8oz*	*240g*
cottage cheese	*2 cup*	*7oz*	*200g*
cream	½ *cup*	*4oz*	*120g*
milk	*1pt*	*16 fl oz*	*4dl*
butter	*2½ tb*	*2 tb*	*2 tb*
sugar	*2½ tb*	*2 tb*	*2 tb*
breadcrumbs	*2½ tb*	*2 tb*	*2 tb*
salt	*1 tsp*	*1 tsp*	*1 tsp*
egg	*1*	*1*	*1*

Bring the milk to the boil and cook the buckwheat till thick. Add the cottage cheese, well drained and rubbed through a fine sieve. Mix well with the buckwheat adding cream. Stir in beaten raw egg, salt and sugar.

Spread in a buttered dish dusted with breadcrumbs, level the surface and brush with melted butter. Bake in a hot oven for 30min; serve with melted butter and cold sour cream.

Rice cutlets

	USA	Imperial	Metric
rice	*1½ cup*	*10oz*	*300g*
eggs	*3*	*3*	*3*
milk	*2 cup*	*16 fl oz*	*4dl*
breadcrumbs	*5 tb*	*4 tb*	*4 tb*
cream	*1½ tb*	*1 tb*	*1 tb*
butter	*2½ tb*	*2 tb*	*2 tb*
olive oil	*½ tb*	*½ tb*	*½ tb*
salt	*1 tsp*	*1 tsp*	*1 tsp*
oil or butter for frying			

Boil the rice in milk (water can be used) 2 fingers above the surface of the rice until it is quite soft. Add salt. Leave until the rice is lukewarm. Mix in the melted butter. Beat 1 whole egg and 1 yolk; add to the rice.

Taking heaped tablespoons of the mixture form into oblong cutlets and coat each with flour. Dip each cutlet into 1 beaten egg mixed with olive oil, then coat thickly with breadcrumbs. Fry in oil or butter until well browned on each side. Serve with mushroom sauce (see p 114).

Gurievskaya kasha (semolina with nuts)

	USA	Imperial	Metric
semolina	*1 cup*	*8oz*	*240g*
walnuts or cob or mixed	*1lb*	*1lb*	*300g*

	USA	Imperial	Metric
bitter almonds	*2*	*2*	*2*
milk, whole (or ⅔ milk and ⅓ cream)	*3pt*	*3pt*	*1½l*
sugar	*1 cup*	*8oz*	*240g*
apricot jam	*as required*	*as required*	*as required*
glacé cherries ⎫ *crystallised fruit* ⎭	*1 cup*	*8oz*	*240g*

Scald the nuts and almonds and remove skin, grind or pound.
Pour the milk into a flat shallow dish and set in moderate oven
until a brown skin is formed on top of the milk. Remove carefully and put to one side on a plate. Repeat the process until
half a dozen skins have been collected.

In the remaining milk simmer the semolina on low heat until
thick, mix in sugar and nuts. Take a deep fireproof dish well
buttered. Spread a layer of semolina, then one of the brown
milk skins, cover with a layer of jam and fruit. Repeat these
layers until the dish is filled. Sprinkle with sugar and breadcrumbs, brown for a few minutes in a hot oven. When cold it
can be coated with icing (confectioner's) sugar which is then
browned under a grill.

9
The Tea-Table

Tea or coffee accompanied by buns and fancy bread, biscuits and creamy cakes is served at some time in late afternoon or evening, depending on the hour set for dinner. Tea is usually served last thing at night but it can also be a kind of 'high tea' in late afternoon with the addition of some zakouski or supper dishes.

No plates of bread and butter feature on the tea table. Before the revolution white bread was considered a luxury and even to this day in many parts of the country it is called 'boulka' (bun) while 'khleb' (bread) refers only to black rye bread.

The central feature of a tea-table is the samovar. In former days it was heated with charcoal but today electric samovars are more general. The samovar is not a tea urn but a receptacle in which water is kept at boiling point. A small tea-pot with very strong tea, of an unscented variety grown in Georgia, Armenia or Azerbaidjan, is set on top of the samovar to keep hot. From it a little tea is poured into the glass, which is then filled up with water from the samovar—kept replenished when necessary. Russian tea is drunk with a slice of lemon, and often enough a spoonful of raspberry, strawberry or blackcurrant jam replaces sugar.

The prianik is the oldest of Russian sweetmeats. Traditionally it is a small cake made with honey and spices (prianosti). Prianiki can also be made with different flavours and resemble a slightly floury meringue. If hot honey or syrup is used in the making, the dough should be left for an hour or two in the refrigerator before baking.

Prianiki with honey and spices (to make 24)

	USA	Imperial	Metric
flour	1½ cup	6oz	180g
eggs	2	2	2
sugar	10 tb	4oz	120g
cinnamon			
nutmeg			
ginger	ground, ¼ tsp each		
cloves			
cardamom			
baking powder	½ tsp	½ tsp	½ tsp
honey	2½ tb	2 tb	2 tb
olive oil	1 tb	1 tb	1 tb

Mix together oil and honey. Beat eggs and sugar until white and fluffy. Sift flour with baking powder and stir in the spices. Gradually mix the spiced flour into the eggs and sugar and then add the honey. The dough should be stiff but not dry. Cool for 1hr in the refrigerator.

Roll into small balls in the palms of your hands and place, well separated, on a greased baking sheet. Bake in a pre-heated fairly hot oven for 20min.

Spiced prianiki are usually glazed while still hot by dipping into a syrup made with 8 tb sugar and 2 tb water, into which is folded a stiffly beaten egg white. Cool on a wire grill.

Mint prianiki (makes 24)

	USA	Imperial	Metric
flour	*1½ cup*	*6oz*	*180g*
caster (granulated) sugar	*1¼ cup*	*8oz*	*240g*
eggs	*3*	*3*	*3*
butter, unsalted	*2½ tb*	*2 tb*	*2 tb*
mint oil	*30 drops*	*30 drops*	*30 drops*
baking powder	*½ tsp*	*½ tsp*	*½ tsp*

Beat the eggs and sugar together until white and fluffy. Gradually mix in sifted flour with baking powder, stir in the mint oil making sure that it is well distributed. Grease a baking sheet with unsalted butter and dust with flour, shaking off the excess. With a teaspoon place rounds of the mixture onto the sheet and bake for 20min in a pre-heated fairly hot oven.

Other flavourings for prianiki instead of mint oil: 1 tb raspberry syrup or else 2 tb rosewater.

Krendel (shaped like a pretzel)

	USA	Imperial	Metric
milk	*½ cup*	*4 fl oz*	*1dl*
flour	*2 cup*	*8oz*	*240g*
egg	*1*	*1*	*1*

	USA	Imperial	Metric
egg yolk	1	1	1
sugar	5 tb	4 tb	4 tb
butter	5 tb	2oz	60g
salt	¼ tsp	¼ tsp	¼ tsp
yeast	½oz	½oz	15g
chopped almonds	2½tb	2 tb	2 tb
icing (confectioner's) sugar	1¼ tb	1 tb	1 tb

NOTE: Raisins, sultanas (white raisins), walnuts and glacé cherries optional.

Dissolve the yeast in warm milk, add half the flour, stir well and set to rise in a warm place covered with a cloth. When the dough has doubled its volume beat the eggs and sugar until white and add to the risen dough with the remaining flour. Knead the dough while adding the melted butter and continue until the dough no longer sticks to the sides of the bowl or the hands—20–30min. Roll into a ball, dust with flour and set to rise again.

When it has once again doubled its volume, set on a floured board and form into a long sausage, thicker and flatter in the centre, tapering towards the ends. Turn the ends in loops to meet in the centre of the roll. Leave on a greased baking sheet to rise for another 30min. Brush the top with melted butter, dust with icing (confectioner's) sugar and sprinkle thickly with chopped almonds. Bake for 30–40min in a medium oven. Be sure to make the loops big enough so that the dough does not merge in baking. The same amount of dough can be used to make two or three small krendels which then take only 15min or so to bake.

I like to add a handful of raisins and sultanas to the dough and decorate the top with walnuts and glacé cherries as well as the chopped almonds.

Almond biscuits

	USA	Imperial	Metric
flour	2 cup	8oz	240g
butter	1 cup	8oz	240g
sugar	1 cup	7oz	200g
almonds	¾ cup	4oz	120g
raisins	½ cup	4oz	120g
egg yolks	6	6	6
salt	¼ tsp	¼ tsp	¼ tsp
lemon oil	4 drops	4 drops	4 drops
orange	½	½	½

Whip 5 egg yolks with the sugar until white. Separately beat the butter to a cream and then mix with the egg and sugar. Gradually add the sifted flour stirring all the time. Mix in raisins, half the chopped almonds, lemon oil and the grated rind from ½ an orange. Stir thoroughly.

Butter a baking sheet and on it thickly spread the dough. Brush with the remaining egg yolk, well beaten, and sprinkle with the remaining chopped almonds. Bake in a fairly hot oven for about 30min. But as soon as the biscuit begins to brown and can be cut without the dough stretching under the knife, withdraw the baking sheet and cut rapidly into squares or oblongs then return to the oven to brown and dry. Cool on a wire grill.

Cinnamon rings

	USA	Imperial	Metric
butter	¾ cup	5oz	150g
sugar	5 tb	4 tb	4 tb
flour	¾ cup	5oz	150g
egg yolks	1	1	1
eggs, hard-boiled	5	5	5
cinnamon	2 tsp	2 tsp	2 tsp
caster (granulated) sugar	1¼ tb	1 tb	1 tb
chopped almonds	1 tb	1 tb	1 tb

Beat butter and sugar till white with chopped hard-boiled yolks and one raw egg. Mix in flour and 1½ tsp cinnamon sifted together. Continue to beat for several minutes. Mix caster (granulated) sugar with ½ tsp cinnamon. Make small rings of the dough and dip some of them in the caster sugar, others brush with milk and sprinkle with chopped almonds. Bake in low oven for 20min.

Boubliki

These are yeast dough rings to be eaten hot with butter or cut in half and toasted.

	USA	Imperial	Metric
flour	1lb	1lb	500g
yeast	¼oz	¼oz	5g
sugar	2 tsp	2 tsp	2 tsp
water or milk	1¼ cup	10 fl oz	2½dl
salt, a pinch			
poppy seed to sprinkle			

Dissolve the yeast and sugar in warm milk or water to which ¼ of the flour has been added. When this starts to rise add the remaining flour and salt. Knead well to form a stiff dough. Roll it into small sausages and join the ends together firmly. Leave to rise in a warm place for 30min. Prepare a pan of fast boiling water, drop in the boubliki one at a time. When they float to the surface remove carefully with a fish slice and set to drain, cool and harden. Sprinkle thickly with poppy seeds and bake on a lightly greased sheet in a hot oven for 20min until crisp and brown.

Lemon air cake

	USA	Imperial	Metric
eggs, separated	5	5	5
sugar	1 cup	7oz	200g
lemon	½	½	½

	USA	Imperial	Metric
cornflour (cornstarch)	2½ tb	2 tb	2 tb
self-raising flour	2½ heaped tb	1½ heaped tb	1½ heaped tb
breadcrumbs	1¼ tb	1 tb	1 tb

Beat yolks with sugar until white. Add juice of ½ lemon and the grated rind of ½ lemon. Mix in the cornflour (cornstarch) and stir until completely blended, then add the ordinary flour. Beat the egg whites until absolutely stiff and fold in. Pour into a buttered cake tin dusted with breadcrumbs. Bake for 1hr in very low oven.

Mazourek with wine

	USA	Imperial	Metric
flour	2 cup	8oz	240g
cream	1 cup	8 fl oz	2dl
sugar	⅔ cup	5oz	150g
butter	1 cup	8oz	240g
egg	1	1	1
mixed peel	1 heaped tsp	1 heaped tsp	1 heaped tsp
lemon juice	1¼ tsp	1 tsp	1 tsp
almonds, chopped	¼ cup	1½oz	50g
caster (granulated) sugar	1¼ tb	1 tb	1 tb
white wine	5 tb	4 tb	4 tb

Mix together flour, cream, sugar, egg, wine, lemon juice and mixed peel to form a dough. Chill in the refrigerator for 30min. Roll into a square and place on buttered baking sheet. Brush the surface with wine, sprinkle with caster (granulated) sugar and chopped almond. Bake in a fairly hot oven. When it begins to brown cut rapidly into triangles or squares. Replace in the oven to dry.

Evgenia tort

	USA	Imperial	Metric
eggs	4	4	4
egg yolks	2	2	2

	USA	Imperial	Metric
sugar	2 cup	14oz	420g
cornflour (cornstarch)	6 tb	5 tb	5 tb
pistacchio nuts	⅓ cup	2oz	50g
almonds	⅔ cup	4oz	120g
mixed peel	1 tb	1 tb	1 tb
whipped cream for filling	1 cup	8 fl oz	2dl

Beat together eggs, yolks and sugar until white and light. Add cornflour, mixed peel, pistacchio nuts and almonds and mix thoroughly. Half the mixture should be very finely chopped or blended, the other half coarsely chopped. Mix both together. Place in 2 buttered medium-sized sandwich pans and bake in moderate oven. Sandwich with whipped cream and cover with chocolate icing or coffee icing using the following ingredients: *Chocolate icing* made from

> 6 tb icing (confectioner's) sugar
> 1 egg white, well-whipped
> 2 tb grated chocolate
> 1 tsp rum
> ½ tsp lemon juice

For *coffee icing* replace the chocolate with 2 tsp of very strong black coffee. Then harden in the refrigerator.

Rum tort

	USA	Imperial	Metric
self-raising flour	1 cup	4oz	120g
butter, unsalted	1 cup	8oz	240g
eggs, separated	2	2	2
sugar	1 cup	7oz	200g
mixed peel	1 tb	1 tb	1 tb
jam, raspberry	5 tb	4 tb	4 tb
rum	2½ tb	2 tb	2 tb

Rum icing

	USA	Imperial	Metric
icing (confectioner's) sugar	1 cup	4oz	120g
rum	1 tb	1 tb	1 tb
lemon juice	2 tsp	2 tsp	2 tsp

Beat butter and egg yolks till light, gradually add sugar, mixed peel and flour. Mix thoroughly. Fold in the stiffly beaten whites. Place in a buttered cake pan and bake for 30min in a moderate oven. Transfer to cake dish and allow to cool. Mix jam with 2 tb rum and spread over the top of the tort. Make icing by mixing icing (confectioner's) sugar, rum and lemon juice. Spread over the tort. Return it to the cooling oven for 10min to harden the icing.

Plain baba with yeast

A tall very light cake made either with yeast or with extremely stiff whipped white of egg. (Old recipes specify the use of 30 eggs to make a yard high baba). Different flavouring can be used such as lemon, almond, chocolate or rum.

	USA	Imperial	Metric
eggs	6	6	6
butter, clarified	1½ cup	12oz	3½dl
yeast	2oz	2oz	60g
flour	2½ cup	10oz	300g
milk	½ cup	4 fl oz	1 dl
sugar	½ cup	4 oz	120g
raisins	1 cup	6oz	180g
currants	½ cup	2oz	60g
cinnamon, a pinch			
salt, a pinch			

Dissolve the yeast in warm milk. Beat the eggs thoroughly and add to the yeast. Stir till blended. Mix in the flour little by little. Beat with a wooden spoon until thick and then knead with hands for about 15min. Cover the dough and set in a warm place to rise for an hour. As soon as it has doubled in volume, knead again, adding the clarified butter spoon by spoon. Still kneading incorporate the raisins, currants, salt and cinnamon.

When thoroughly blended, place in a high cake pan which should not be more than ⅓ filled. Cover with a cloth and set in a warm place for another hour. Bake in a hot oven on the middle rung. After 10min, lower to a moderate heat and bake for 45min or until cooked through when tested with a fine knife.

Cover the top loosely and allow to cool for 15min before removing from tin. If no tall cake ring is available make one by adding a stiff paper band round the existing one (as one might for a soufflé).

Chocolate baba without yeast

	USA	Imperial	Metric
eggs, separated	8	8	8
flour	½ cup	3oz	150g
sugar	1 cup	8oz	240g
chocolate, grated	10 tb	4oz	120g
vanilla essence	4 drops	4 drops	4 drops
breadcrumbs	14 tb	4oz	120 g

Beat the egg yolks with sugar until fluffy, gradually add breadcrumbs and vanilla. Beat until smooth. When the mixture has thickened and is pale add the grated chocolate and flour. Beat till blended. Whip the egg whites till they stand in peaks and fold lightly into the mixture. Place in a cake ring and bake as in previous recipe.

Rum baba

Take a plain baba while still warm and lay on one side in a dish with rum syrup made of:

	USA	Imperial	Metric
sugar	1 cup	7oz	350g
water	2 cup	1pt	½l
rum	5 tb	4 tb	4 tb

Make a syrup of the sugar and water, add the rum when the sugar is dissolved and the water reduced. Allow to cool. Baste the baba with the syrup turning it over and spooning up the

syrup that runs off, until all has been soaked in. When the baba is quite cold cover the top with rum icing (see p 181).

Sweet pirog

Sweet pirog (or tart) is usually made of short crust pastry. For a medium-sized flan ring, the following ingredients are required:

	USA	Imperial	Metric
flour	*1½ cup*	*6oz*	*180g*
butter	*½ cup*	*4oz*	*120g*
caster (granulated) sugar	*4 tb*	*2oz*	*60g*
egg yolk	*1*	*1*	*1*

Make a hollow in the middle of the flour and add the softened butter, sugar and egg yolks. Mix well, sprinkling with water to form a stiff dough.

Bake the flan case blind in the oven and then fill with any kind of jam or fruit: apple purée with black cherry jam; a layer of raspberry jam to hold a mixture of raw fruit—plum, pear, peach, apricot, cherry etc; black cherry jam topped with whipped cream; apple purée with chopped roasted almonds.

Baked cream and cherry pirog

The favourite way of cooking a sweet pirog is to bake the fruit (morello cherries, blackcurrant or bilberry) together with the shortcrust pastry.

	USA	Imperial	Metric
fruit	*2 cup*	*8oz*	*240g*
sugar	*8 tb*	*3oz*	*90g*
double (heavy) or sour cream	*½ cup*	*4 fl oz*	*1dl*
shortcrust pastry (see above) to			
which is added 1 tb lemon juice			

Prepare the pastry mixing in the lemon juice. Roll it out fairly thick especially round the rim of the flan which should be slightly above the ring itself. Mix the fruit with the sugar and cover the surface of the pastry. Pour on the cream. Bake in a medium oven for 30min.

During the cooking the fruit and cream melt into the pastry forming a delicious combination. The fruit and cream are bubbling as the flan is removed from the oven and it should be left to cool and set before removing from the ring.

SWEETS

Iced cranberries

	USA	Imperial	Metric
cranberries	*1lb*	*1lb*	*500g*
icing (confectioner's) sugar	*1 cup*	*4oz*	*120g*
egg white	*1*	*1*	*1*

Whip the egg white till it stands in peaks and fold in the sugar to form an icing. Dip each cranberry individually to coat and place one by one on a baking sheet in a cool oven for 15min or until the icing has set.

Tyanushki (a soft fudge)

	USA	Imperial	Metric
lump sugar	*1lb*	*1lb*	*500g*
cream	*2 cup*	*16 fl oz*	*4dl*
vanilla	*4 drops*	*4 drops*	*4 drops*
lemon juice	*2 tsp*	*2 tsp*	*2 tsp*
rose water	*1 tb*	*1 tb*	*1 tb*

Bring all the contents to the boil in a pan and continue boiling, with the pan on an asbestos sheet, for 45min, stirring at intervals. When the mixture is thick, and has coloured, turn out onto a flat dish greased with unsalted butter or vegetable fat. Cool. Cut into small oblongs with a very sharp knife. Each sweet should be slightly gummy in the centre. The longer the mixture cooks the more crumbly it becomes.

Caramel chestnuts

Roast the required number of chestnuts, remove shells and as much skin and fibre as possible. Pin a nut one at a time with a skewer and dip into hot thick caramel syrup made with browned sugar and a little water. Drain off the excess syrup and stand the chestnuts on a buttered sheet to harden.

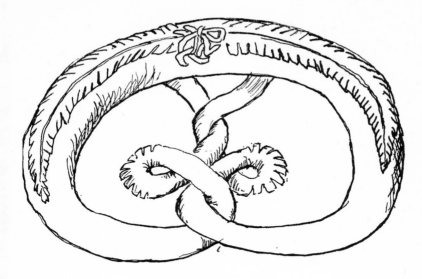

Apple pastila

This can be made of any kind of fruit juice boiled to form a jelly.

	USA	Imperial	Metric
cooking apples	*2lb*	*2lb*	*1k*
caster (granulated) sugar	*1½lb*	*1½lb*	*750g*
egg whites	*3*	*3*	*3*
ground almond	*5 tb*	*1oz*	*30g*
rosewater	*2½ tb*	*2 tb*	*2 tb*
vanilla essence	*1 tsp*	*1 tsp*	*1 tsp*

Cook the apples, quartered and cored but not peeled, in enough cold water to cover, until the apples are soft and transparent. Strain through a cloth squeezing out all the juice. To each measure of apple juice add the same measure of sugar. Boil softly until the mixture thickens and jells when tested on an iced spoon. Add ground almonds, rosewater, vanilla and stiffly beaten egg whites. When blended add one more measure of sugar and continue to cook, stirring constantly, until thick.

Transfer to a greased dish in a layer about 1in thick. Smooth the surface and set in a very cool oven for 2–3hr to dry. When it is firm enough, cut into oblongs and coat with sugar. Return to the oven for 30min to harden.

10

Festive Tables

In former days observance of the long weeks of Lent was strictly
enforced by the tenets of the Orthodox Church. Not only meat
but any animal produce such as eggs, milk, butter, lard were
prohibited in the preparation of food.

In Russia, as in most of the countries of Europe, a carnival
marked the last days before Lenten severity. This was called

'Butter Week' (Maslenitsa) and was celebrated by the cooking of bliny, small pancakes made from yeast batter. As the word 'Easter' derives from the name 'Eastre', a Teutonic spring goddess, so are pancakes supposed to originate in a pagan rite to celebrate the sun by baking replicas of his golden orb.

Bliny, usually eaten at midday dinner, were a meal in themselves. A clear borschok would be served first, followed by a dish of bliny, steaming under a napkin—this first contingent to be followed by a succession of others until no more could be eaten. There would be a competition among the younger members of the family as to how many bliny could be consumed—ten, twenty, forty . . .

Bliny are served with bowls of cold sour cream and sauce boats of melted butter. In addition they are accompanied by caviar, salted cucumbers, pickled mushrooms, marinaded fruit, salted herrings, smoked salmon, and followed by a very cold sweet or an assortment of fruit.

Bliny are traditionally made with buckwheat flour alone or half and half with ordinary flour. However plain flour can be used just as well.

Bliny (to serve 8)

	USA	Imperial	Metric
flour	4 cup	1 lb	500g
milk	3 cup	1¼ pt	7 dl
clarified butter	10 tb	8 tb	8 tb
yeast	1 oz	1 oz	30g
sugar	1 tsp	1 tsp	1 tsp
cream	6 tb	6 tb	6 tb
salt	1 tsp	1 tsp	1 tsp
eggs	3	3	3

NOTE: One should not use smaller quantities if bliny are to succeed but the batter keeps well in a refrigerator for two or three days for future use.

Warm part of the milk and dissolve the yeast. Mix with half the flour and stand in a warm place for 2hr to rise. When it has doubled in volume add the rest of the flour, rub together the sugar and egg yolks till white and add to the dough. Stir in the remaining milk and salt. Mix well and put batter back in a warm place to rise once again.

Whip the egg whites till stiff and separately whip the cream. Fold the whipped whites into the cream (not vice versa) and mix with the batter just before using.

Heat small, lightly buttered pans and cook the bliny which should be slightly thicker than ordinary pancakes. As soon as one side is browned brush the other surface with clarified butter and turn. Wipe the pan between each pancake to remove impurities, never using water on the pan.

Lent ended with the midnight mass on Easter Saturday. The Easter table would be set in readiness for the return from church. In the villages the women would take their paskhas and cakes to church with them to be blessed. Easter meant three traditional foods: paskha (the same word as 'Easter' in Russian) which is a rich sweet pyramid of curds and cream; koulitch a tall dry Easter cake to counteract the richness of the paskha; and coloured hard-boiled eggs. It was a custom at Eastertime to exchange coloured eggs with friends and neighbours, a custom which evolved into painting intricate designs on the hard-boiled eggs, then into exchanging painted wooden or porcelain eggs and culminated in the elaborate jewelled and enamelled masterpieces produced by Fabergé.

An Easter table would be laden with cold ham, fish in aspic, vegetable salads, salted cucumbers, pickled mushrooms, caviar, pirog, fresh and marinaded fruit as well as vodkas and wines. Koulitch and paskha would be eaten all through Easter week.

Paskha (serves 8–10)

A paskha is shaped in a 4-sided wooden Turks-head mould with a small opening at the narrow end to drain off any moisture. Since these special moulds are not readily available, most Russians now use a fairly large clay flower-pot—long and narrow if possible—which is smoothly lined with two or three layers of butter muslin, leaving an overhang of several inches to fold over.

There are a number of ways of making paskha which vary in richness ie in the amounts of egg and cream included, or whether the paskha is cooked or made of raw ingredients, white or 'pink' ie coloured with raspberry jam. The following recipe is for the standard, uncooked paskha.

	USA	Imperial	Metric
curd or cottage cheese	3lb	3lb	1½kg
sour cream, or double (heavy) cream	½ cup	4oz	1dl
unsalted butter	1 cup	8oz	240g
almonds	⅔ cup	4oz	120g
glacé cherries	⅔ cup	4oz	120g
candied peel	⅔ cup	4oz	120g
raisins, seedless	1 cup	6oz	180g
eggs	3	3	3
caster (granulated) sugar	1 cup	7oz	200g
rosewater or vanilla essence	1 tsp	1 tsp	1 tsp

The cottage cheese must be absolutely dry before use. Hang in a muslin bag for 12hr or else place in a colander under a heavy weight. When dry, rub through a fine sieve into a basin. Keep some almonds and glacé cherries for decoration, chop the others and then mix with the cottage cheese, together with raisins, softened butter, vanilla essence and candied peel. Whip the eggs and sugar together and add. Beat thoroughly until no lumps remain. Then, stir in cream, but do not use an electric blender.

When throughly beaten and absolutely smooth pour into the mould lined with butter muslin. Fold the ends of the muslin over the top, cover with a small plate to distribute the weight and weigh down with anything heavy standing narrow end downwards in a deep plate in the refrigerator for another 12hr. When removed from the refrigerator a lot of moisture will have drained out. Undo the butter muslin, place on a flat dish and turn over, carefully removing the mould. Decorate with almonds and glacé cherries. 'XB' used to be outlined on one side, indicating the words 'Christos Voskress' (Christ is risen) and a paper rose would decorate the summit.

It is an excellent sweet for a cold buffet but must always be accompanied by some dry not too sweet bun or sponge such as koulitch (see p 194).

Koulitch

	USA	Imperial	Metric
flour	4lb	4lb	2kg
yeast	2oz	2oz	60g
butter, clarified	1¼ tb	1 tb	1 tb
milk	3½ cup	1½pt	1l
eggs	5	5	5
sugar	3 cup	1½lb	750g
vanilla essence	1 tsp	1 tsp	1 tsp
saffron	1 tsp	1 tsp	1 tsp
currants	1½ cup	8oz	240g
ground almonds	1 cup	8oz	240g
roasted almonds, for decoration			

Dissolve the yeast in a little warm milk and make a dough with half the flour. Knead well for 15min. Cover with a cloth, set in a warm place to rise, leave for 1 hr.

Add half the remaining flour, melted butter, milk, beaten eggs, sugar, currants, almond, saffron and vanilla. Knead well until the dough is firm and all ingredients blended. Cover and leave overnight.

In the morning add the remaining flour. Knead for 15 or 20min and place dough in a buttered round medium-sized cake pan with a thin stick upright through the centre of the dough. The dough should fill approximately a third of the pan. Leave it to rise in a warm, draughtproof place until it nearly fills the entire tin. Bake in a hot oven for 1hr, test by inserting a fine knife to see that the koulitch is baked through.

Lay on one side to cool, turning at times so that the koulitch retains its straight baba-like shape. When cold, decorate the top with roasted almonds, and a little white icing.

Koulitch is sliced horizontally, the top being replaced each time to keep it fresh. Each round is then cut into four or six pieces as desired.

11

Caucasian Cooking

Caucasian cookery is quite unlike the Russian. The three Transcaucasian republics of Georgia, Armenia and Azerbaidjan have a subtropical climate and extremes of temperature varying from mountain ranges with their high summer grazing for sheep and their trout-filled torrents, to the low-lying areas of humid heat where citrus fruits and rice and tea are grown. Vineyards cover the foothills of Georgia and Armenia producing the red Mukuzani and white Tsinandali from Georgia and the dozen or more varieties of cognac which Armenia can boast. Fruit of all kinds abounds and is eaten at any time of day. Vegetables and salads form an important part of every meal. Food is generally spicy with garlic and herbs and peppers to wet lagging appetites in hot exhausting days. Rice and cracked wheat are the predominant cereals and lamb the prevailing meat. Cool plates of yoghourt accompany nearly every dish.

Traditionally food was prepared outside—on spits, in clay ovens, in pots over open fires. To preserve it, meat would be dried in the hot sun, whilst dried fruit such as apricots and raisins are constantly used as flavouring. Probably the one single ingredient to appear most often in Caucasian recipes are walnuts—chopped or ground—which grow wild in every region.

ZAKOUSKI

Zakouski to accompany the local 'raki' (instead of vodka) are salads of different vegetables in which aubergines (eggplants) and sweet peppers play a predominant part. Cheeses made from goat's or ewe's milk, yoghourt and spring onion or even a selection of raw herbs eaten with bread or a dish of delicious sesame seed dressing called Tahina (obtainable in tins or bottles in large delicatessens).

Tahina and spinach (with thanks to Ashkhain Atikian)

	USA	Imperial	Metric
spinach	1lb	1lb	500g
tahina	½lb	12oz	360g
lemon	1 large	1 large	1 large
garlic	2 cloves	2 cloves	2 cloves
paprika	1 tsp	1 tsp	1 tsp
salt, pepper, to taste			

Wash the spinach and remove stalks (or use frozen spinach). Chop and boil for 10min then drain well, so that the spinach is dry, and then mash. Crush the cloves of garlic and mix with the spinach, season to taste and stir in the tahina. Add the juice of the lemon and mix throughly. At first the tahina thickens but mix hard until the desired consistency for a dip is reached.

Sprinkle with paprika. This dip is delicious with hot flat bread (see p 218).

Thin slivers of raw carrot can be placed round the dip both as decoration and to eat with it.

If tahina is unobtainable ready made, it can be produced by mixing 10 tb sesame seeds in a cup of water, 2 crushed cloves of garlic, juice of 2 lemons, salt and pepper in an electric blender until it is the consistency of thick mayonnaise.

Aubergines with yoghourt and garlic

	USA	Imperial	Metric
aubergines (eggplants)	*4*	*4*	*4*
oil	*2 tb*	*2 tb*	*2 tb*
sweet pepper	*1*	*1*	*1*
garlic	*1 clove*	*1 clove*	*1 clove*
lemon juice	*5 tb*	*4 tb*	*4 tb*
yoghourt	*½ cup*	*4 fl oz*	*1dl*
salt, a pinch			

Bake the aubergines (eggplants)—done on hot coals in Armenia —cool and peel. Brown each aubergine all over in hot oil in a frying pan, sprinkle with salt and pour 1 tb of lemon juice over it. Mince or very finely chop together the sweet pepper and garlic and then liquidise or pound. Put the pounded pepper in a dish or deep plate, on it lay the aubergines and cover with yoghourt. Stand in the refrigerator until very cold.

String bean and walnut salad

	USA	Imperial	Metric
string beans	*½lb*	*½lb*	*240g*
ground walnut	*4 tb*	*1oz*	*30g*
vinegar	*2½ tb*	*2 tb*	*2 tb*
chopped parsley	*2½ tb*	*2 tb*	*2 tb*
salt, pepper, to taste			

String, chop and cook the beans in salted water. Drain and

cool. Transfer to a salad bowl, mix with vinegar, season and stir in the ground walnuts. Top the salad with finely chopped parsley or any other herbs such as tarragon or marjoram.

Khmoropatik (asparagus fritters)

	USA	Imperial	Metric
asparagus	*1lb*	*1lb*	*500g*
For batter:			
flour	*2 cup*	*8oz*	*240g*
water	*½ cup*	*4 fl oz*	*1dl*
oil	*3 tb*	*2 fl oz*	*½dl*
salt, to taste			

Prepare the asparagus, removing the hard stalks, and boil in salted water for 25min. Drain well and cut into medium-sized pieces. Prepare a batter with the flour, water and oil. Coat each piece of asparagus and deep fry. Drain well and serve cold.

Kololik of red haricot beans

	USA	Imperial	Metric
haricot beans	*¾lb*	*12oz*	*360g*
ground walnut	*16 tb*	*4oz*	*120g*
onion	*2*	*2*	*2*
cranberries	*1 cup*	*3oz*	*90g*
salt, pepper, to taste			

Boil the haricot beans in salted water until quite soft, drain and then sieve to make a purée. Mix with finely chopped raw onion, ground walnuts, stoned cranberries and seasoning to taste. Moisten the mixture slightly with a little of the water in which the haricots were boiled, so that it can be rolled into balls the size of a walnut. Arrange these on a dish and sprinkle with finely chopped herbs.

SOUPS

In the Caucasus soups are thick and nourishing enough to form a meal in themselves. In some regions there is so little liquid in the soup that it is what might well be termed a stew.

Bozbash (lamb soup)

	USA	Imperial	Metric
breast of lamb	1lb	1lb	500g
potatoes	2 large	2 large	2 large
onion	1	1	1
oil	2½ tb	2 tb	2 tb
tomato	¾lb	12oz	360g
string beans	¼lb	4oz	120g
sweet pepper	1 small	1 small	1 small
aubergine (eggplant)	2	2	2
courgettes (zucchinis)	2 small	2 small	2 small
coriander basil parsley	1 tsp each		
salt, pepper, to taste			

Cut the breast of lamb into small pieces (about 16) and simmer in water until half cooked, periodically skimming off the fat. Remove the meat from the stock and fry in oil until browned. Strain the stock. Add potato and aubergine (eggplant) diced, onion chopped and fried, courgettes (zucchinis) left whole with stalk removed and sliced sweet pepper. Simmer until the vegetables are cooked. Fifteen minutes before serving add seasoning, herbs and quartered tomatoes.

Fruit msapur (made with lamb)

	USA	Imperial	Metric
stewing lamb	1lb	1lb	500g
apple or quince	¾lb	12oz	360g
onion	3	3	3

	USA	Imperial	Metric
prunes	½ *cup*	*4oz*	*120g*
tomato purée	2½ *tb*	*2 tb*	*2 tb*
flour	1¼ *tb*	*1 tb*	*1 tb*
sugar	1¼ *tb*	*1 tb*	*1 tb*
water	*2pt*	*2pt*	*1l*
oil	½ *tb*	½ *tb*	½ *tb*
salt, to taste			

Cut the meat into pieces and fry in oil together with the diced onion. Add 6 tb water, cover with a lid and simmer for 15min. Slice the peeled and cored apples, chop the stoned prunes and put into the pan with the meat. Simmer until they are cooked. Pour on water. Brown the flour with the tomato purée, mix in the sugar and stir into the soup. Season to taste and simmer for a further 10min.

Ddmapur (pumpkin or squash soup with meat balls)

	USA	Imperial	Metric
bones for stock	*1lb*	*1lb*	*500g*
minced (ground) beef	½*lb*	*8oz*	*240g*
pumpkin or squash	*2lb*	*2lb*	*1kg*
onion	*1 large*	*1 large*	*1 large*
oil	*10 tb*	*8 tb*	*8 tb*
egg	*1*	*1*	*1*
water	*3pt*	2½*pt*	1½*l*
salt, pepper, to taste			

Simmer the bones for 1hr in the water. Strain. Peel the squash, remove seeds and cut into small cubes. Fry the chopped onion in oil. Mix the minced (ground) meat with egg, salt, pepper and a pinch of dried herbs (dill, marjoram, lovage) then roll into balls the same size as the pieces of squash. Put squash, fried onion and meat balls into the strained stock and simmer for 10–15min until the squash and meat balls are cooked.

Chkhritma (chicken soup with saffron)

	USA	Imperial	Metric
chicken	*1 small*	*1 small*	*1 small*
egg yolks	*2*	*2*	*2*
onion	*½lb*	*½lb*	*240g*
butter	*5 tb*	*2oz*	*60g*
flour	*4 tb*	*1oz*	*30g*
white wine vinegar	*1 tb*	*1 tb*	*1 tb*
ground saffron	*2 tsp*	*2 tsp*	*2 tsp*
coriander	*sprig*	*sprig*	*sprig*
salt, pepper, to taste			

Prepare the *infusion of saffron*: place the saffron in a small bowl and cover with boiling water. Stand, covered, in a warm place for 2hr. Strain. The liquid should be dark golden-brown in colour and scented.

Meanwhile boil the chicken in enough water to cover. Strain the stock and cut the cooked chicken meat in pieces. Fry the chopped onion in butter, brown the flour and dissolve in a little chicken stock. Return pieces of chicken, fried onion and flour to the strained stock and bring to the boil.

Beat the two yolks in a bowl adding warm stock gradually so that the eggs do not curdle. Add the infusion of saffron, chopped coriander and wine vinegar. Stir into the soup just before serving, not allowing the soup to boil. Lamb can be used instead of chicken.

Wedding soup with arishta (vermicelli)

	USA	Imperial	Metric
chicken	*1 small*	*1 small*	*1 small*
onion	*2 medium*	*2 medium*	*2 medium*
carrot	*3*	*3*	*3*
egg yolks	*3*	*3*	*3*
lemon juice	*2½ tb*	*2 tb*	*2 tb*
parsley	*2½ tb*	*2 tb*	*2 tb*
arishta	*½lb*	*½lb*	*240g*

Finely chop the onion and carrot and boil in a pan with the chicken covered in water, until 2½ pints strong chicken broth remains. Season to taste and strain. Put the arishta (see next recipe) into the strained stock. Cook until soft (15min). Beat the yolks, gradually adding the lemon juice and stir into the soup just before serving together with the chopped parsley.

Arishta

	USA	Imperial	Metric
wheat flour	*1lb*	*1lb*	*500g*
eggs	*3 medium*	*3 medium*	*3 medium*
water	*½ cup*	*4 fl oz*	*1dl*
salt	*1 tsp*	*1 tsp*	*1 tsp*

Sieve the flour into a mound, make a hollow in the centre and put in the eggs, water and salt. Knead until a very firm dough is formed. Divide the dough into 3 or 4 pieces, roll out very thinly and then roll up into a tight sausage. Slice this into thin slices, unroll into strands, dry for 10 min in a very low oven and keep in an airtight container.

FISH

Fish is not abundant in the Black Sea, therefore Georgia and Armenia rely mainly on the several kinds of trout to be found in the swift mountain streams.

Trout with walnut sauce (served hot or cold)

	USA	Imperial	Metric
trout	4	4	4
For sauce:			
ground walnuts	½ cup	4oz	120g
sugar	1¼ tb	1 tb	1 tb
salt	1 tsp	1 tsp	1 tsp
vinegar	4 tb	2 fl oz	½dl
chopped coriander and parsley	2½ tb	2 tb	2 tb
water	1 cup	8 fl oz	2dl

Salt the prepared trout both inside and out, then simmer in a closed fish pan with water ¼ up the fish for 15min. Remove carefully with a fish slice so as not to break the fish.

Prepare the sauce meanwhile: simmer the ground walnuts, salt and sugar for 10min in water. Add the vinegar and chopped herbs and simmer for a further five minutes. Pour over the fish.

Trout stuffed with tarragon

	USA	Imperial	Metric
trout	4	4	4
white wine	1 cup	8 fl oz	2dl

	USA	Imperial	Metric
tarragon	5 tb	4 tb	4 tb
spring onion, chopped	1 cup	7oz	300g
plum or apricot (fresh or dried)	½ cup	2oz	60g
pomegranate seeds	1 cup	8oz	240g
salt, paprika, to taste			

The belly of the fish should not be slit but the fish cleaned through the openings left after the removal of the gills. Rinse the fish well, rub the inside with salt and paprika and stuff with chopped tarragon, chopped spring onion and fruit. If no fresh tarragon is available mix 4 tsp dried tarragon with some bread soaked in milk, chopped onion and beaten egg.

Fasten the tail of the stuffed fish through the opening in the lower jaw and then simmer for 15–20min on a trivet in white wine.

The trout, eaten hot or cold, are served with pomegranate seeds.

MEAT

Ashtarak tolma (apples or quince stuffed with lamb)

	USA	Imperial	Metric
lamb	*1lb*	*1lb*	*500g*
rice	*2 tb*	*10z*	*30g*
apples	*4 large*	*4 large*	*4 large*
quince	*4 large*	*4 large*	*4 large*
onion	*1 large*	*1 large*	*1 large*
dried apricot and prunes	*½ cup*	*3oz*	*90g*
sugar	*1¼ tb*	*1 tb*	*1 tb*
herbs, mixed	*1¼ tb*	*1 tb*	*1 tb*

Boil the rice for 15–20min. Mince the meat. Mix the meat and rice with finely chopped onion and herbs, salt to taste.

Cut the tops off the apples and quince and carefully remove the core leaving a fairly roomy hollow. Sprinkle the inside with a little sugar and then stuff with the minced (ground) lamb. Put the tops back onto the fruit and stand them in a large saucepan with dried prunes and apricots in between the fruit.

Pour some stock halfway up the apples, weigh down with an inverted plate and cover the pan firmly with a lid. Simmer on low heat for 40min until cooked through.

Kchoutch (casseroled lamb with dried apricot)

	USA	Imperial	Metric
lamb (from leg or shoulder)	*1lb*	*1lb*	*500g*
potatoes	*4*	*4*	*4*
string beans	*½lb*	*½lb*	*240g*
dried apricot	*¾ cup*	*4oz*	*120g*
tomatoes	*½lb*	*8oz*	*240g*
garlic	*½ clove*	*½ clove*	*½ clove*
sweet pepper	*1*	*1*	*1*
onion	*1 medium*	*1 medium*	*1 medium*
aubergines (eggplants)	*6*	*6*	*6*
mixed herbs	*2½ tb*	*2 tb*	*2 tb*

Dice the peeled potatoes, slice the onion in rings, chop the sweet pepper, crush the garlic and halve the tomatoes. Put all these in a casserole with the dried apricot and the meat cut into fairly large pieces. Sprinkle with mixed herbs (marjoram, tarragon, dill), and barely cover with water.

Cook in a firmly lidded casserole in a fairly hot oven for 2hr. Halfway through the cooking add the aubergines (eggplants) cut into pieces and season to taste.

Shashlyk

This, primarily Caucasian dish, has become such an integral part of Russian cooking that I have earlier given the classic recipe (see p 100). Shashlyks vary according to the size of the pieces of meat to be barbecued and the accompaniments to the dish. (In an Armenian cookery book a recipe for 'shepherd's khorova' starts with the words 'skin the carcase of a young ram'.)

Summer shashlyk

Summer shashlyk, for instance, is prepared the same way as on p 100 but is accompanied by a couple of aubergines, (eggplants), a sweet pepper and several tomatoes per person cooked on separate spits and then peeled and served with the meat sprinkled with chopped spring onion or chives.

Shashlyk po karski

This is a speciality of Nikita's Restaurant in London, to whom I am indebted for the recipe.

	USA	Imperial	Metric
saddle of lamb cut into			
½*lb pieces*	*4 pieces*	*4 pieces*	*4 pieces*
lamb kidneys	*4*	*4*	*4*
vinegar	*10 tb*	*8 tb*	*8 tb*
lemon	*1*	*1*	*1*

	USA	Imperial	Metric
brandy	*4 tb*	*4 tb*	*4 tb*
onion	*½lb*	*½lb*	*240g*
cloves	*8*	*8*	*8*
fennel, parsley, dill	*1 sprig each*	*1 sprig each*	*1 sprig each*
(or heaped tsp dried)			
salt, pepper, to taste			

Place the lamb in an earthenware bowl, sprinkle with salt, juice from half the lemon, pepper, and brandy. Grate half the onion and cover the meat, add cloves and leave to marinade for several hours, turning occasionally. Halve the kidneys, removing the membrane. Thread first half a kidney, then the marinaded meat, then the other half of the kidney onto a spit and cook over hot charcoal, turning frequently so that the meat is evenly cooked. Serve with slices from the remaining lemon and rice.

In the Caucasus instead of kidney they sandwich the meat between large pieces of 'kurdiuk', which is a fat from the tail of one particular breed of lamb and is considered a great delicacy.

Moussaka (braised beef with squash)

	USA	Imperial	Metric
rump steak	*1lb*	*1lb*	*500g*
squash	*2lb*	*2lb*	*1kg*
butter	*6 tb*	*3oz*	*90g*
rice	*⅓ cup*	*2oz*	*60g*
tomatoes	*½lb*	*8oz*	*240g*
onion	*¼lb*	*4oz*	*120g*
salt, pepper, to taste			

Cut the steak into fairly small cubes and fry on all sides in butter until browned. Put in a casserole, just cover with water and braise until soft. Meanwhile boil the rice for 10–15min until about half cooked. Chop and fry the onion and mix with the rice. Peel the squash, remove seeds, slice it fairly thickly and brown in butter.

Mix the cooked meat with the rice and onion, season with salt and pepper. In a buttered fireproof dish spread first a layer of squash then the meat and rice and cover with the remaining squash. Surround with halved tomatoes, moisten with some of the liquid in which the meat was cooked and finish cooking in a medium oven for 15min.

Pork and quince

	USA	Imperial	Metric
lean pork	*1lb*	*1lb*	*500g*
quince	*12oz*	*12oz*	*360g*
clarified butter	*7½ tb*	*6 tb*	*6 tb*
cloves	*4*	*4*	*4*
cinnamon	*½ tsp*	*½ tsp*	*½ tsp*
salt, pepper, to taste			

Cut the pork into 4 pieces, sprinkle with salt and pepper and fry until well browned on all sides. Slice the peeled and cored quince and cook in butter until it begins to soften. Put the meat into the centre of a casserole and surround with quince, add the cloves and sprinkle with cinnamon. Moisten with the butter from the frying pan diluted with 8 tb water. Cover the casserole with a lid and braise for ½hr in a medium oven.

Pheasant in wine

	USA	Imperial	Metric
pheasant	*1*	*1*	*1*
white wine	*1 cup*	*8 fl oz*	*2 dl*
butter	*½ cup*	*4oz*	*120g*
salt, pepper, to taste			

Salt the pheasant inside and out and brown all over in butter. Place in a casserole, pour the wine over the bird and cover firmly with a well fitting lid. Simmer for 1hr on very low heat and serve with its own gravy. Serve with marinaded grapes and fried potatoes.

Chicken tapaka

	USA	Imperial	Metric
young chicken	*4 small*	*4 small*	*4 small*
or	*2 medium*	*2 medium*	*2 medium*
butter	*7 tb*	*5 tb*	*70g*
tomatoes	*½lb*	*8oz*	*240g*
aubergines (eggplants)	*¼lb*	*4oz*	*120g*
sweet pepper	*1 small*	*1 small*	*1 small*
garlic	*1 clove*	*1 clove*	*1 clove*
salt, pepper, to taste			

Remove the legs of the chickens from below the drumstick and cut the bird down the breast bone so that it can be spread-eagled. Flatten with one or two taps of a cleaver. Fasten the ends of the legs and wings firmly in the loose skin of the sides so that a compact piece results. Sprinkle with salt and pepper.

Melt the butter in a pan and put in the chickens to cook keeping them flat in the pan by laying a weighted plate on them. Fry for 20–25min each side until brown.

Simmer together the chopped aubergines (eggplants), sweet pepper and tomatoes with the crushed garlic. Sprinkle with parsley and serve round each portion of chicken.

VEGETABLES

These are extremely popular in the Caucasus where beetroot (beet) and cabbage and salted cucumber are replaced by squash and aubergines (eggplants), asparagus and tomatoes while walnut is as frequent an ingredient as the Russian sour cream. Garlic and onion are used a great deal. Chopped garlic sprinkled over a deep plate of yoghourt features at practically every meal.

Squash or *pumpkin* is served in a great variety of ways: it is cooked in milk or baked in the oven stuffed with nuts and raisins; it is simmered with lentils and fried onion or baked like a pudding with sugar and cracked wheat.

Fried squash

Peel the squash and remove the seeds. Slice fairly thinly and sprinkle each slice with salt and pepper. Coat each slice in flour (breadcrumbs can be used if preferred) and then fry gently in melted butter until soft. Serve with yoghourt and finely chopped garlic.

String beans and mixed vegetables

	USA	Imperial	Metric
string beans	*1lb*	*1lb*	*500g*
onion	*1 large*	*1 large*	*1 large*
tomatoes	*4 medium*	*4 medium*	*4 medium*
sweet pepper	*1 small*	*1 small*	*1 small*
vinegar	*1¼ tb*	*1 tb*	*1 tb*
water	*½ cup*	*4 fl oz*	*1dl*
sunflower oil	*1¼ tb*	*1 tb*	*1 tb*
salt, pepper, to taste			

Slice and cook the beans in salted water. Drain. Fry the chopped onion in sunflower oil, put in a pan with the beans, sliced tomatoes, chopped sweet pepper, and seasoning. Pour on the vinegar diluted in hot water and simmer for 20min.

Aubergines with almonds and walnut sauce

	USA	Imperial	Metric
aubergines (eggplants)	*1lb*	*1lb*	*500g*
ground almonds	*5 tb*	*4 tb*	*4 tb*
oil	*1¼ tb*	*1 tb*	*1 tb*
vinegar	*1¼ tb*	*1 tb*	*1 tb*
salt, pepper, to taste			

Peel the aubergines (eggplants), remove the seeds from the centre and slice them in rings. Sprinkle with salt and leave for 15min for the liquid to come to the surface. Squeeze off the excess liquid and fry in oil. Sprinkle with vinegar, cover each slice with ground almonds and serve with walnut sauce (see p 204).

Mushroom khmoropatik (deep fried fritters)

	USA	Imperial	Metric
mushrooms	*½lb*	*8oz*	*240g*
oil	*1 tb*	*1 tb*	*1 tb*
flour	*12 tb*	*4 oz*	*120g*

	USA	Imperial	Metric
egg	*1*	*1*	*1*
milk	*1 cup*	*8oz*	*2dl*
soda	*pinch*	*pinch*	*pinch*
salt	*½ tsp*	*½ tsp*	*½ tsp*
lemon	*1*	*1*	*1*

Wash and peel the mushrooms and simmer for 5min in a very little boiling water. Drain, cool and slice. Prepare the batter: whip the egg with salt, oil, soda and flour. Stirring constantly dilute with milk to the consistency of thick cream.

Dip each slice of mushroom in the batter and deep fry in hot fat until browned. Serve with quarters of lemon.

Asparagus bake

	USA	Imperial	Metric
asparagus	*1lb*	*1lb*	*500g*
spring onion	*1 bunch*	*1 bunch*	*1 bunch*
eggs	*2*	*2*	*2*
melted butter	*8 tb*	*6 tb*	*6 tb*
lemon	*1*	*1*	*1*
saffron	*2½ tsp*	*2 tsp*	*2 tsp*
parsley	*1 sprig*	*1 sprig*	*1 sprig*
salt, pepper, to taste			

Prepare the asparagus, cutting off the hard ends, and boil in salted water. Drain and cut into small pieces.

Chop the spring onion and parsley; fry in melted butter. Mix with the asparagus. Make an infusion of saffron (see p 202) and add to the asparagus with salt and pepper to taste. Place the asparagus mixture in a buttered fireproof dish and pour on the well beaten eggs. Bake in a medium oven until the eggs are set. Serve with quarters of lemon.

Walnut omelette

	USA	Imperial	Metric
eggs	6	6	6
walnut kernels	½ cup	2oz	60g
melted butter	5 tb	4 tb	4 tb
cinnamon	1 pinch	1 pinch	1 pinch
salt, pepper, to taste			

Beat the eggs with a fork and mix in the chopped walnuts. Melt the butter in an omelette pan, pour on the beaten eggs seasoned with salt and pepper. Cook for about 5min until the omelette is ready. Sprinkle with cinnamon and serve.

Pilaff

All pilaffs are made with a basis of rice and are among the main dishes in the Caucasus. Rice for pilaff is prepared as follows:

	USA	Imperial	Metric
rice	1½ cup	8oz	240g
water	2pt	2pt	1l
salt	2½ tsp	2 tsp	2 tsp
melted butter	8 tb	6 tb	6 tb

Cook the rice in boiling salted water until the grains are softening but not cooked through. Drain the rice in a fine sieve and rinse well in warm water.

Melt the butter in a deep pan and gradually pour in the rice, stirring until each grain is coated. Cover the pan firmly and stand on very low heat for 45min until cooked through.

This pilaff is served with any kind of omelette, with fresh peas or cooked dried haricots, mixed with caraway seeds or fried mushrooms, with fried chicken and with trout.

Pilaff with fried lamb

	USA	Imperial	Metric
rice	1½ cup	8oz	240g
melted butter	8 tb	6 tb	6 tb

	USA	Imperial	Metric
lamb	1lb	1lb	500g
onion	2	2	2
pomegraniate seeds	½ cup	4oz	120g
salt, pepper, to taste			

Prepare the rice as in the previous recipe. Cut the meat into small pieces and brown all over. Chop and fry the onion and mix with the meat together with pomegranate seeds. Just cover with water and braise gently until soft. Add salt and pepper and serve round the rice.

Pilaff Ararat

	USA	Imperial	Metric
rice	1½ cup	8oz	240g
melted butter	8 tb	6 tb	6 tb
apples	7	7	7
quince	4	4	4
sultanas (white raisins)	1 cup	6oz	180g
almonds	½ cup	3oz	90g
dried apricots	1 cup	4oz	120g
brandy	3 tb	3 tb	3 tb
sugar	½ cup	3oz	90g
salt, to taste			

Prepare the rice as on p 214. Set aside 3 apples and bake the 4 apples and 4 quince cored and sugared in a hot oven (if no quince is available apples can be used instead). Roast the blanched and peeled almonds, soak the dried apricots for 30min and then chop and fry in butter together with the sultanas.

When all is ready make a mound of the rice on a dish and cover halfway up from the base with the sultanas, apricots and chopped roast almonds, so that it resembles the snow-covered peak of the mountain. Arrange the baked fruit round the base and among them place the three raw apples, which have been cored and hollowed, with the tops removed. Into each hollowed apple pour 1 tb of brandy. Set the brandy alight and serve, having first extinguished all lights in the room.

Korket (cracked wheat)

	USA	Imperial	Metric
cracked wheat	½ cup	4oz	120g
onion	2 large	2 large	2 large
melted butter	¾ cup	6 fl oz	1½dl
water	2pt	2pt	1l
salt	1 tsp	1 tsp	1 tsp

Soak the wheat for half an hour in cold water and drain. Pour the wheat into fast boiling salted water, add 2 tb melted butter, bring the water up to the boil and then simmer for about 30min until the wheat is cooked and the water absorbed. Chop and fry the onion, mix with the cooked wheat and serve with melted butter. (May be used instead of rice.)

SWEET

Caucasians do not generally have a sweet after food. Fresh fruit or cheese is the usual ending to a meal, followed by tea or coffee with a dry yeast gata or some biscuits and nuts. Maybe a very sugared sweetmeat such as halva or gozinakh may be passed round. They are, however, great makers of jam to eat with flat unleavened bread and jams are made from all fruit and berries, rose petals, squash and melon, aubergine (eggplant) and walnut. But they do prepare some sweets:

Arkandj (Armenian pancake)

	USA	Imperial	Metric
flour	2 cup	8oz	240g
egg yolks	3	3	3
salt	1 pinch	1 pinch	1 pinch
brandy	4 tb	4 tb	4 tb
butter	½ cup	4oz	120g
caster (granulated) sugar	2 tb	2 tb	2 tb

Beat together the egg yolks and brandy, gradually add the flour and mix into a soft dough. Divide the dough into 4 pieces and roll out into very thin rounds. Make 3 incisions on the surface and fry in boiling butter until each side is a light golden colour. When ready, drain off the excess butter and sprinkle heavily with sugar.

The pan in which the pancakes are cooked should be slightly smaller than the diameter of the pancake.

Walnut marbles

	USA	Imperial	Metric
flour	½lb	8oz	240g
butter	½ cup	4oz	120g
yoghourt	½ cup	4oz	120g
eggs	2	2	2
soda	½ tsp	½ tsp	½ tsp
sugar	¾ cup	6oz	180g
vanilla	¼ tsp	¼ tsp	¼ tsp
walnut kernels	1¼ cup	8oz	240g
caster (granulated) sugar	2 tb	2 tb	2 tb

Beat the eggs into the yoghourt, add soda and melted butter. Stir well, gradually adding the sifted flour. Stand the dough in the refrigerator for 30min.

Chop the walnuts and mix with a little sugar.

Roll out the dough very thinly and divide into squares. Place some nut filling in the centre of each square and pinch the edges together firmly, rolling to form a ball. Place on a buttered sheet and bake in a hot oven for 35min. When the marbles are cool, sprinkle with caster (granulated) sugar.

Lavash (flat Armenian bread)

It should be baked by slapping the thin round pieces of dough onto the sides of a red hot cylindrical stove ('tonir') when it takes less than 5min to bake. Lavash has practically no crumb and can keep for a month if stored in an air-tight tin.

	USA	Imperial	Metric
flour	*5 cup*	*1½lb*	*750g*
warm water	*2 cup*	*16 fl oz*	*4dl*
dried yeast	*½ tsp*	*½ tsp*	*½ tsp*
sugar	*1 tsp*	*1 tsp*	*1 tsp*
salt	*2 tsp*	*2 tsp*	*2 tsp*

Mix together the flour, sugar and salt. Make a hollow and into this pour the yeast dissolved in ½ cup of warm water. Stirring all the time gradually add the rest of the water and knead until the dough no longer sticks to the hands. Cover the ball of dough with a cloth and stand in a warm place to rise for 3–4hr. Divide the dough into six portions and roll out very thinly to fit the baking sheet which should not be greased. Preheat the oven to moderate temperature and bake for about 30min until crisp and coloured.

Gozinakh (honey and walnut sweetmeat)

	USA	Imperial	Metric
walnut kernels	*½lb*	*8oz*	*240g*
honey	*½lb*	*8oz*	*240g*
sugar	*5 tb*	*2oz*	*60g*

Chop the walnuts and lightly roast them. Boil together the honey and sugar and mix in the walnuts. Boil for 15min. Moisten a dish with cold water and pour out the mixture. Level the surface and cool. Remove the gozinakh by slightly warming the dish and cut into small squares.

Liqueur apricots

Fill glass jars with firm ripe apricots, cover the fruit with brandy and leave to macerate for two days at least. Pour off the brandy. Make a thick syrup in the proportion of $1\frac{1}{2}$ caster sugar to 1 of water. Add brandy or rum to taste and pour over the apricots.

Marinades and Beverages

Instead of pickles Russians like fruit and vegetables in a marinade, which is not so sharp as a pickling solution. Marinades are served with meat or fish, either hot or cold. White wine vinegar or else cider vinegar should be used, avoiding the strong flavour of malt vinegar. The vinegar, diluted with water, together with the other ingredients in the marinade recipe, should always be brought to the boil and only used when cold. Marinades do not keep as long as pickles.

Marinaded grapes, cherries, redcurrants or plums

	USA	Imperial	Metric
fruit	*2lb*	*2lb*	*1kg*

	USA	Imperial	Metric
Marinade			
vinegar	*1 cup*	*8 fl oz*	*2dl*
water	*2 cup*	*16 fl oz*	*4dl*
sugar	*1 cup*	*7oz*	*200g*
salt	*1 tsp*	*1 tsp*	*1 tsp*
oil to seal	*1 tb*	*1 tb*	*1 tb*

Pack the stoned and stalked cherries or plums into jars (grapes and currants are left in clusters). Cover with the marinade, previously boiled and cooled. Pour some oil on the surface of the marinade to seal. Cover the jars firmly and store. Ready to use after 3 weeks.

Marinaded melon (served with roast meat)

	USA	Imperial	Metric
melon	*1 large*	*1 large*	*1 large*
Marinade			
vinegar	*1 cup*	*8 fl oz*	*2dl*
water	*1 cup*	*8 fl oz*	*2dl*
sugar	*½ cup*	*4oz*	*120g*
honey	*2½ tb*	*2 tb*	*2 tb*
cloves	*3*	*3*	*3*
cinnamon	*½ tsp*	*½ tsp*	*½ tsp*
peppercorns	*8*	*8*	*8*
salt	*½ tsp*	*½ tsp*	*½ tsp*

Boil the marinade, strain and cool. Peel the not over-ripe melon and and remove the seeds. Cut the melon flesh into cubes and pack into sterilising jars. Put on the covers and boil in a steriliser for 1hr then allow the jars to cool in the water. Store in a cool place.

Marinaded pears

	USA	Imperial	Metric
pears	*2lb*	*2lb*	*1kg*

	USA	Imperial	Metric
Marinade			
vinegar	*1½ cup*	*12 fl oz*	*3dl*
sugar	*½ cup*	*3½oz*	*100g*
cloves	*4*	*4*	*4*
cinnamon	*1 tsp*	*1 tsp*	*1 tsp*
salt	*½ tsp*	*½ tsp*	*½ tsp*

Peel the pears thinly, leaving them whole. Stand in a pan, cover with water and simmer gently until soft. Remove the pears from the liquid without breaking.

Into the hot liquid put vinegar, sugar and spices. Bring to the boil. Return the pears to the pan and boil up two or three times in the marinade. Pack away in jars and cover with the strained marinade.

Soused apples

Select perfect apples and place in layers in a large jar or small cask, with blackcurrant leaves (or cherry leaves) between each layer of apples, also fresh tarragon and basil (optional). If no fresh herbs available boil up some dried herbs in the saline solution of 2 tb salt to 2 pints water. Bring to the boil three times and cool. Cover the apples with the cold solution and immediately seal the jar or cask. Keep in a cold place for a month before use.

Marinaded cabbage

	USA	Imperial	Metric
hard white cabbage	*2lb*	*2lb*	*1kg*
salt	*1 tb*	*1 tb*	*1 tb*
Marinade			
vinegar	*1 cup*	*8 fl oz*	*2dl*
water	*2½ cup*	*1½pt*	*½l*
sugar	*1 cup*	*7oz*	*200g*

	USA	Imperial	Metric
peppercorns	6	6	6
bayleaf	3	3	3
oil to seal			

Boil the marinade with all ingredients except the oil. Cool. Chop the cabbage finely, rub well with salt and leave to stand for 10min. Squeeze off the moisture and pack into jars. Cover with the cold marinade, pour a little oil on the surface of each jar, to seal. Store in a cool place. Ready for use after a week. Excellent in salads.

Marinaded beetroot (beet) (used for Borsch)

	USA	Imperial	Metric
beetroot (beet)	*2lb*	*2lb*	*1kg*
Marinade			
vinegar	*1 cup*	*8 fl oz*	*2dl*
water	*2 cup*	*16 fl oz*	*4dl*
sugar	*1¼ tb*	*1 tb*	*1 tb*
salt	*½ tsp*	*½ tsp*	*½ tsp*
peppercorns	*6*	*6*	*6*
cloves	*3*	*3*	*3*
bayleaves	*2*	*2*	*2*

Prepare the marinade with all the ingredients, bring to the boil and cool. Boil the unpeeled beets and leave them in the water to cool. When cold, peel and cut into cubes. Pack into jars and cover with the cold marinade. If used for borsch, the marinade replaces vinegar in the recipe.

Marinaded mushrooms

	USA	Imperial	Metric
mushrooms	*2lb*	*2lb*	*1kg*
salt	*2 tb*	*1½ tb*	*1½ tb*
vinegar	*1 cup*	*8 fl oz*	*2dl*
water	*1 cup*	*8 fl oz*	*2dl*

	USA	Imperial	Metric
bayleaf	*1*	*1*	*1*
pepper			
cloves } *ground*	*¼ tsp each*	*¼ tsp each*	*¼ tsp each*
cinnamon			
dill, seed or weed	*1 tsp*	*1 tsp*	*1 tsp*
oil to seal			

Clean and stalk the mushrooms, put in a pan with the water, vinegar and salt; bring to the boil. Skim off any froth and add spices, bayleaf and dill weed. Simmer for 20min, stirring at intervals so that all the mushrooms are equally cooked through. Leave until quite cold before transferring to jars together with the strained liquid. Pour a little oil onto the surface of each jar to seal and stand for a couple of days in the refrigerator before storing.

Dried mushrooms

Dried mushrooms are widely obtainable commercially. Personally I prefer the large mushrooms sold by weight, off strings, to the smaller, broken ones in plastic packets. Dried mushrooms may appear more expensive then fresh, but they are so light that only one or two are required for flavouring. Furthermore they provide a variety of taste, as they include many kinds rarely found on sale. In certain large food stores specific types can be bought separately, such as dried chanterelles or dried cèpes.

Dill-pickled cucumbers

This is a misnomer, since these cucumbers are preserved in brine without any vinegar. They are easily prepared at home with small ridge cucumbers, and the fresher the cucumber, the better the result.

Stand the cucumbers on end in a glass jar between layers of blackcurrant leaves and dill. Cover with cold brine made of 3 tb salt to 2 pints water. These are ready for use after four days.

Rapidly salted cucumber

This can be produced in a few hours by either cutting off the ends of ridge cucumbers or else using pieces of long hot-house cucumbers (which enables the brine to penetrate rapidly). Cover with hot brine made as in the previous recipe. Allow to cool and then chill in the refrigerator before using.

BEVERAGES

Russians are renowned as tea-drinkers and on p 175 is a detailed explanation of how to use a samovar. The tea-drinking habit is succinctly illustrated on the railways. Train journeys in Russia tend to be long—overnight is usual and it takes up to eight days between Moscow and Vladivostok. In each coach travels a conductor in charge of the passengers and the samovar.

Every two or three hours he comes round with glasses of tea, at a minimal charge payable at the end of the journey. The experienced traveller always comes provided with lemons and a knife to slice them with.

Coffee has become a popular drink, especially since the introduction of instant coffee. It is only in Russia however, that I have seen coffee offered with lemon. It turned out to be a delicious drink: a tumbler of black coffee with some sugar and a slice of lemon floating in the glass.

Beer, vodka and cognac are the most popular alcoholic drinks. The beer is of a continental 'lager' type and is of various kinds: 'Leningrad' (the most expensive), 'Moscow', 'Jigouli' or 'Zolotaya Raketa'.

Vodka (see p 18) is a strong, colourless spirit distilled from rye, barley or oats. It is practically tasteless unless flavoured with herbs. The vodkas found in shops in the Soviet Union are Stolichnaya in various degrees of proofing, Kristall, Extra, Osobaya and a mature smooth vodka called Starka. Among vodkas produced outside the Soviet Union the best that I have tasted is Vladivar (known as 'the vodka from Varrington') which I can thoroughly recommend. Vodkas with different flavours are hot and peppery Pertsovka, Zubrovka which has the picture of a bison on the label and a strand of buffalo grass in the bottle, Petrovskaya and Okhotnichnaya which are both flavoured with different herbs. It is quite easy to flavour vodka if desired by putting a twist of orange or lemon peel in the bottle and leaving it for a few hours. If tied with a thread the peel is then easily removed, as too long immersion makes it bitter.

In the Soviet Union both vodka and cognac are sold by the gramme—100 grammes being about 4 fluid ounces. *Cognacs* are produced in the Caucasus where one finds numerous Armenian varieties and the best known Tbilisi brandy. Moldavian cognacs are also excellent.

Table wines also come from the Crimea and the Caucasus, both dry and semi-sweet. There is red Mukuzani and Sapiravi,

Naparaouli, Kinsmaouli and very popular Khvanchara which is sold by the glass at refreshment counters in theatres and department stores. Also popular are the white Tsinandali, Goudjouani, Eneseli and rather sweet Tvishi.

Champagne is not expensive and can be bought by the glass. It is a highly refreshing drink in the bustle and heat of an over-crowded shopping centre. Strangely, Russians prefer sweet champagne which is therefore more expensive then dry.

Kvass, a fermented rye bread drink tasting of weak beer is sold from containers in the streets (see p 55). Often enough home-made kvass is produced with various berries or fruit, covered with boiling water and fermented for a few weeks with sugar, honey and sultanas.

Fruit juices of all kinds are widely used. In the home, drinks prepared with fresh fruit are popular.

Fresh peach and melon drink

Cut the melon and peach flesh in cubes, sprinkle with lemon juice and sugar. Chill in the refrigerator. Serve in tall glasses with soda water and a pinch of ground ginger.

Fruit punch

A mild form of punch is also a favourite summer drink: sprinkle chopped fruit or berries with a little sugar, add a few tablespoons of brandy and leave to macerate for several hours. Transfer to a jug and pour on champagne or white wine with the same quantity of fresh lemonade. Stand in the refrigerator and serve very cold.

An old fashioned but still popular drink, which I well remember being served to my grandmother as a mid-morning pick-me-up, is

Gogol-mogol (to make 1 portion)

	USA	Imperial	Metric
egg, separated	*1*	*1*	*1*
sugar	*1¼ tb*	*1 tb*	*1 tb*
salt	*1 pinch*	*1 pinch*	*1 pinch*
wine	*2½ tb*	*2½ tb*	*2½ tb*
milk	*¾ cup*	*6 fl oz*	*1½dl*

Whip the egg yolk and sugar, add salt and mix in the wine. Pour into the milk, stir, strain and then add to the stiffly beaten white of egg.

Sweet gogol-mogol

The above can be served as a sweet (rather like zabaglione) with sponge fingers. In which case double the amount of sugar, whip stiff with the white of egg. Add wine, milk and 1 tb of brandy. Serve topped with whipped cream.

Acknowledgements

My thanks to Shura Shihwarg for his encouragement and help, Jo Fitzlyon for her drawings, Ashkhain Atikian for her Caucasian expertise and Clarice Bourchier for patient and meticulous typing.

Besides recipes garnered over the years, I have consulted the following: *Podarok Molodoi Khozaike* by Elizaveta Molokhovetz (St Petersburg, 1896); *Koulinarnye Retsepty* (Moscow, 1956); *Kniga o Vkousnoi i Zdorovoi Pische* (Moscow, 1965); and *Armianskaya Koulinaria* (Moscow, 1971).

Index

235